The Devil's Disciple

Bernard Shaw

The Devil's Disciple

edited by
Margery Morgan

Longman

LONGMAN GROUP UK LIMITED
Longman House
Burnt Mill, Harlow, Essex CM20 2JE, England
and associated companies throughout the world.

First published 1984
Sixth impression 1993
ISBN 0 582 33092 0

Produced by Longman Singapore Publishers Pte Ltd
Printed in Singapore

The publisher's policy is to use paper manufactured from
sustainable forests.

Contents

A personal essay

by John Russell Brown

The plays of Bernard Shaw

I have never known what to say about the plays of Bernard Shaw, and never been quite certain how to study them. I sometimes think that I enjoy them too much.

Perhaps I should begin by stating the obvious. According to the standards of practical and profitable theatre, Bernard Shaw is one of the greatest dramatists in the whole world. At first he experienced difficulty in having his plays performed because of censorship or because he could not get an appropriate theatre or the right cast to perform them. *Widowers' Houses*, which he started to write in 1884, was the earliest to be produced, but it was put on by J T Grein's Independent Theatre Society in 1892 for only two special performances. But now, more than ninety years since he decided to write for the stage and more than thirty since his death in 1950, Bernard Shaw can pack theatres in every English-speaking nation and in many others besides.

He wrote more than fifty plays of varying length, and more than a dozen of them have been renowned successes almost from the first. Their star parts have attracted the very best actors of each generation and have proved responsive to many changes of fashion, thought and social expectations. The passage of time has not rendered them obsolete but discovered new strengths, unexpected comedy and further subtleties of characterization. Shaw's dialogue, especially, has remained immediately accessible – animated, fascinating and apparently new-minted.

Not all the plays we enjoy today were received at first with acclamation. Some press criticisms of *Androcles and the Lion*, after its first production in 1913, are representative in their variance from each other:

A very discursive and ill-knit play, which is, moreover, bound to give offence to not a few ...

The Morning Post

A really bright and brilliant piece of work, not half so portentous as Mr Shaw can be when he likes ...

The Daily Chronicle

Even while we laughed we had some qualms of conscience ...

The Daily Telegraph

Laughter long and loud vollied and even thundered in the St James's Theatre last night. It was not the cynical, ill-natured laughter that often marks a Shaw première, but merriment – glad, spontaneous and uncontrolled ...

The Evening Standard

The present play is not even up to the level of *Caesar and Cleopatra*, by no means one of Shaw's best efforts ...

The Daily Herald

In late life Shaw used to say that each one of his plays was hailed as a masterpiece, except the last one. He quoted a critic's description of him as 'a dignified monkey shying coconuts at a bewildered public', and professed to be 'touched' at the softening adjective, 'dignified'.

Bernard Shaw did not make it easy for his critics, because he never stopped drawing attention to himself, telling others what to think and cultivating an arresting public *persona* that was somewhat comic and occasionally tiresome. In part this may be due to spending all his early years as an outsider: a naturally curious boy, dissatisfied at school; an Irishman in exile; an unpublished novelist; a bachelor until the age of forty-two. He had come to London from Dublin in 1876 at the age of nineteen, having already worked as a land-agent's clerk for more than four years. Now he was joining his mother and sister in order to become a writer, but he earned only a pittance for ten industrious years before gaining recognition. Not until 1887 did the fourth of his novels become the first to be published in book form.

The very titles of these works suggest their writer's long and self-conscious pursuit of success and of his own proper place in life: *Immaturity, The Irrational Knot, Love Among the Artists, Cashel Byron's Profession* (he was a pugilist), *An Unsocial Socialist.* The last of these reflects Shaw's membership of the Fabian Society which dated from 1884 and led to immediate and frequent engagements as a public speaker. In support of this socialist group's determination to 'reconstruct society', he addressed whatever public he could find, on Clapham Common or in small meetings of sympathizers. He gained in exchange a ready turn of clear-sounding phrase, a tone of conviction and a keen sense for the reactions of an audience. All this new experience and new company was valuable to the alert and hard-working writer, and may well have precipitated his movement towards the stage. At about the same time he started to work as a book reviewer and soon afterwards made a name for himself as a weekly music critic and drama critic. When he was thirty-six his first play was produced.

Bernard Shaw was so long in finding his true profession as a dramatist that it seems quite natural that he never lost a youthful zest for this work, retaining into his nineties a love of experiment, fantasy and the unexpected. Almost all his plays raise the questions of dramatic propriety that would have been avoided by any ordinarily accomplished writer. Why should an Epilogue bring back the Dauphin some twenty-five years after the end of *Saint Joan*, so that the Maid can appear to him in a 'pallid greenish light' to be followed by various other 'visions'? Why tie up every minute circumstance in *Arms and the Man* and leave so much in the air at the end of *Pygmalion*, especially when every reader of the text is told what happens after the fall of the curtain in an Epilogue? Is it only an extravagant whim – it could not be inexperience or lack of respect for financial problems – that calls for a taxicab to arrive on stage to carry off Eliza Doolittle at the end of Act I of *Pygmalion*? Why demand two elaborate time-consuming changes of the set in the middle of Act I of *Caesar and Cleopatra* so that a short dialogue can take place while the characters are standing between the paws of the sphinx in the middle of the desert?

Mrs Patrick Campbell, the first Eliza in *Pygmalion*, used to call the play's author 'Joey' as if he were a clown; but that, like Shaw's own public fooling, was nowhere near a full indication of the man or of his plays. Other admirers – and himself in certain moods – could see 'GBS' as a prophet, a topical political thinker. (The Prime Minister and Leader of the Opposition came to see a play he wrote about the state of Ireland.) He tackled large and timely issues such as the future of Christianity, the terrors and attractions of war, the possibility of international disarmament and the role of a poet in society. He wrote *Man and Superman* about evolution and the function of what he called 'The Life Force'; and he published this play with an Epistle Dedicatory – and explanatory – together with a *Revolutionist's Handbook and Pocket Companion*. In the five parts of *Back to Methuselah*, Shaw moved the action from 4004 BC through the centuries to 31,920 AD, which he said was 'As Far As Thought Can Reach'. He published a collection of 'Trifles and Tomfooleries', but he also caused the critics to class him with Ibsen as a supreme Dramatist of Ideas.

Indeed Shaw's plays are full of ideas, discussed at considerable length by their characters and effecting the development of those characters and the situations in which they are presented. No one could miss the author's concern with contemporary politics, morality, science, sociology, education, religion, history, philosophy, bureaucracy and sexuality. He went to great lengths to elaborate his notions further in prefaces, statements and free-ranging essays. He used the occasion of publishing a dramatic text to address his readers on 'Parents and Children', on 'Diabolonian Ethics', 'Better Than Shakespear?' and other topics arising in the plays. He is often so opinionated in the statements these prefaces make about the plays that he may mislead the reader. (There is, of course, no preface when the play is staged in a theatre.) A very brief example is this 'explanation' of an early comedy:

THE PLAYS OF BERNARD SHAW

In *The Philanderer* I have shewn the grotesque sexual compacts made between men and women under marriage laws which represent to some of us a political necessity (especially for other people), to some a divine ordinance, to some a romantic ideal, to some a domestic profession for women, and to some the worst of blundering abominations, an institution which society has outgrown but not modified, and which 'advanced' individuals are therefore forced to evade.

It can be very inhibiting to actors and directors to read such passages, and to read Shaw's elaborate stage directions, which were not intended for them but to help readers who could not see the play and had to make do with a printed text. Imaginative stage interpretation and careful reading of the plays themselves will often bring out further, and perhaps different, meanings not allowed for in Shaw's dogmatic assertions. (I recommend readers to turn to the prefaces only when they are thoroughly familiar with the plays they accompany.) Shaw himself confessed that particular ideas were only a secondary element in a thoroughly good play. When he was asked to contribute to a symposium on 'Should social problems be freely dealt with in the Drama?', he conceded that topical ideas could give an immediate interest to a play, but he went on to stress that they are not necessary. Age, love, death, accident, and 'personal character' all lie outside social institutions, but it is these that give permanent interest to drama, independent of period or place.

In one of his reviews, reprinted in *Our Theatres in the Nineties*, Bernard Shaw wrote that 'people's ideas, however useful they may be for embroidery, especially in passages of comedy, are not the true stuff of drama, which is always the naïve feeling underlying the ideas'.

There is a paradox here which can only be understood by realizing that Shaw's own 'naïve feelings' were dominated by a passionate desire to understand, to be intellectually in control of feeling, laughter, and happiness, as well as argument. He wanted a drama that reflected his own sense of being most alive when in pursuit of some idea or action in which he could have absolute faith. In this he was a resolute romantic, a writer in quest of some secret that was always eluding him. Many of the plays express such an involvement directly:

Everything I think is mocked by everything I do.

Arms and the Man

I think I'm going to die for God. Nothing else is real enough to die for. – What is God? – When we know that, Captain, we shall be gods ourselves.

Androcles and the Lion

What is life but a series of inspired follies? The difficulty is to find them to do.

Pygmalion

I'm always expecting something. I don't know what it is; but life must come to a point sometime.

Heartbreak House

But a single character can never speak wholly for this dramatist: he gave self-confidence and uninhibited clarity to each one of his *dramatis personae* so that the excitement of a play is especially in their *inter*play. Innocence is offset by expediency, personal inspiration by corporate wisdom, deceit by honesty, practicality by vision. The typical ending of Shaw's greatest plays is a moment of balance: sometimes between two people, as in *Man and Superman*; or, more often between a larger grouping, as in *Heartbreak House*, *Pygmalion*, *You Never Can Tell*, and *Candida*. *Saint Joan* concludes with the words of the Maid alone, but these come at the end of an Epilogue which has surveyed a great stretch of European history; they are, perhaps, the most generalized expression of this romantic sentiment:

O God that madest this beautiful earth, when will it be ready to receive Thy saints? How long, O Lord, how long?

Underlying the plays, in all their fantasies, jokes, surprises, provocations and serious argumentations, is their author's passionate insecurity, his unfulfilled desire to understand the whole business and absurdity of life around him, to know what it is like to see with each person's eyes and feel with each person's senses and intelligence. But he is not a gloomy romantic and optimism usually shines through. When Shaw shows men killing each other or submitting to injustice or self-denial, the play is never quite at an end: a joke, a shift of time or a change of focus alters any situation he is able to imagine. He draws audiences into theatres because he shares the exhilaration of his own endless passion to understand.

I have referred frequently to audiences and theatres with good reason. On the page, the plays of Bernard Shaw cannot easily exert their full fascination and this is the prime difficulty of studying them. His writing is so lucid and his vocabulary so simple that it is easy to avoid reading him as attentively as he deserves. His contemporaries, Henry James and W B Yeats, and many other authors a good deal younger than himself, such as D H Lawrence, James Joyce, T S Eliot or Virginia Woolf, wrote in styles that are very obviously of great complexity, depth, originality and subtlety, and they put readers at once upon their mettle and challenge comprehension. In contrast, the style of 'GBS' is un-poetic, and his most brilliant passages are perfectly comprehensible. (The public speaker and the journalist are evident here.) The first step towards a proper appreciation of Shaw is to realize that all his dialogue is designed to be understood as part of the actors' performances. Its subtlety and depth are revealed only in action, infused with feeling and individual reality as the whole play comes to life. Shaw's style should be described as music written for several carefully contrasted instruments, each with its individual tone and requiring an individual instrumentalist.

This does not mean that actors can appreciate readily what comes to a reader only with difficulty. Shaw was quick to agree that his plays needed very special acting and that great virtuosity was required for their 'sudden transitions of mood'. He told a director that his chief task would be to prevent actors taking their tone and speed from one another and 'thus destroying the continual variety and contrast which are the soul of liveliness in comedy and truth in tragedy'. He saw his works as traditional but, at the same time, out-of-fashion because they required larger-than-life performance. He called for a response to his texts similar to that given to Italian and German opera:

> I went back to the classical style and wrote long rhetorical speeches like operatic solos, regarding my plays as musical performances precisely as Shakespeare did.

He was 'furiously opposed' to Pinero, Henry Arthur Jones, Oscar Wilde and other contemporary playwrights who sought realistic speech for their characters: in his view, they pretended to present a picture of life on stage, but placed nothing there but a collection of 'clockwork mice' and 'chemical rabbits'.

Any student of Shaw's plays should try to see them acted by the very best performers when they have got the full measure of their parts. (Actors find that rehearsals of Shaw are very difficult indeed, until they catch the right sound or tempo or pitch to release the truth and vitality of their roles.) In default of that, we should try to imagine the lively interplay of a play's speeches and actions, not read them through silently at a great pace, enjoying simply the art of a master storyteller and stopping only for the very few words that we may not fully understand. Reading a whole play aloud will not be very much help either, although Shaw used to start rehearsals by doing just that himself for his cast. The strong dynamics of the writing must be appreciated. To achieve that it is better to spend a lot of time in reading just one introductory or lively scene and then re-reading it again and again, at first slowly and then more quickly, but always attempting as strong a contrast as possible in speed, tone, manner *and* pitch, between each and every speech. Then it should be possible to introduce transitions within some of the individual speeches, until the whole scene strikes hard and clear with the shafts of Shaw's invention – and ricochets with their splinters. A more difficult, but equally necessary task would be to take one of the long 'arias' and mark that out with a comparable vocal variety and vivacity. Such experiments need a great deal of mental energy and may lead to wild and whirling words, as well as some loss of sense; but the basic qualities of Shaw's dramatic style are almost sure to be discovered in the process.

Of course more than fireworks are needed to bring the plays alive in our imaginations. A commitment must be given to each character in each scene, every moment he or she is on stage: only then will a full flowering occur. Laurence Olivier found the character of Sergius in *Arms and the Man* a 'stupid, idiot part', difficult and thankless to perform. But then, after a performance, the director Tyrone Guthrie said to him 'But don't you love Sergius?' From that moment Olivier no longer thought that he had simply to conform, to provide the cues for Shaw's ideas: '. . . it clicked, and something happened, I suppose, that gave me a new attitude . . . that had been completely lacking in me' (from *Great Acting*, BBC, edited by H Burton). Shaw's letters to the actors and actresses who played his major roles – Mrs Patrick Campbell, Ellen Terry, George Alexander, Louis Calvert and Sybil Thorndike are only a few of the more famous – all show a concern to get things 'right' and to engage the imagination of the performers fully. His disappointments were expressed with equal vehemence: when *Major Barbara* was running at the Court Theatre, London, he sent a message to Charles Wyndham and Mary Moore in New York:

I am afraid I shall have to withdraw it unless you both come and play for me, for nothing else can save that terrible last act.

It can be done but we have not got anywhere near it yet.
(from *All on Stage* by Wendy Trewin, Harrap)

When a whole cast responds to Shaw's musical, muscular writing, when the rhetorical and argumentative points are made clearly, firmly and lightly, when jokes, feelings, thoughts and fantasies are played with complete belief and every role is given its utmost individual worth, then these plays exhilarate and delight. To appreciate them as we read, we must try to imagine all that: and Shaw's writing is so devised that we shall find the adventure is easier than it sounds, and gets easier and more irresistible with practice. In the process we shall find that there is so much we want to say about the plays of Bernard Shaw that it is hard to know where to begin.

Introduction

Shaw's background and early career

The Devil's Disciple was written in the first decade of Shaw's long career as a dramatist. It is an interesting and original play and has a history of success in the theatre, but it is not one of his greatest works. It has some of the qualities of a young man's play, although Shaw was over forty when he wrote it. He had come rather late to the making of plays, after a prolonged attempt to establish himself as a novelist and then a much more successful entry upon professional journalism. Born and, after a fashion, brought up in Dublin in a far from pious Protestant family, he had come to London at the age of nineteen to rejoin his mother, who had left his father and taken her daughters with her. Shaw was deeply attached to his mother and took great pains, in later life, to protect her good name from possible slurs. He has left the impression that she was in some ways a very tolerant woman (though she had not been tolerant of her husband's alcoholism and the way it let down the family socially), perhaps because her passion for music left her little emotion to waste on other matters. Certainly she appears to have left her son much to his own devices or to the care of servants, while they were in Dublin; she was more occupied with her daughters, of whom the elder became a singer in light opera. Mrs Shaw was obviously a woman of some ability, independence and courage, who made her living in London by giving singing lessons to private pupils and teaching music in the North London Collegiate School. Bernard Shaw lived with her and was financially supported by her for ten years of his adult life, while he educated himself in informal ways, wrote novel after novel, became involved in politics, and hardly ever earned any money.

The novels mostly got published, rather obscurely, if only in serial form in a socialist magazine, but they did not bring Shaw fame or money. The best known of these is *Cashel Byron's Profession*, which has been re-published as a Penguin book in recent years. They are all clever and, for much of their length, very lively and entertaining, but uneven in quality. However, it was as a brilliant journalist, witty, often savage, often wildly amusing, that Shaw first impressed himself vividly on a reading public. He was ready to comment on anything and everything, though he was first engaged on a regular basis as a music critic, reviewing concerts and operatic performances: from 1888 for *The Star* newspaper, under the pen-name of Corno di Bassetto, and two years later for *The World*, writing under his own name – or, rather, signing articles with his initials, G.B.S. He started writing for *The Saturday Review* about the plays put on in London from 1895, and he was still doing so while at work on *The Devil's Disciple*.

Becoming a dramatist

Although he had tried his hand at writing plays before, his career as a dramatist began with *Widowers' Houses*, a play he wrote specially for production by the Independent Theatre Society, a group of enthusiasts for the disturbing new drama being produced on the continent of Europe. The Society's productions were occasional and private, for members only, necessary because many of the plays they wanted to mount had no hope of escaping the net of legal censorship, exercised through the office of the Lord Chamberlain. In other instances, they provided a showcase for plays that were too 'advanced', or unconventional, in form and style, to be risked by the commercial managements of the day which, as ever, were chiefly intent on giving the public works that kept to tried-and-tested formulas. *Widowers' Houses* (1892) and *Mrs Warren's Profession* (1894), written for a similar group, the Stage Society, were very serious plays with a strong political drive, though lightened with wit and humour. Both were attacks on the capitalist system as the source of widespread social evils. *Mrs Warren's Profession*, especially, pulled few punches in the way it equated capitalist economy with the management of a chain of brothels.

Capturing a wider audience

Shaw realized that, if he was to reach a wide audience, he had to make compromises. He must not defy the censorship in open and obvious ways; he must capture and hold the attention of people who went to the theatre simply for entertainment, and try to make them see some of the social and political follies in which they were involved. In order to achieve this he had to offer them the kinds of play already popular in the theatre. However, he had to do better than the hack authors already writing for the stage in the freshness, vitality and amusing qualities of what he wrote. In doing this, he was not abandoning any deeply held principles; he was simply presenting them in a different, more generally acceptable, way. He knew very well that seriousness did not have to be dull. He loathed dullness himself, and no one ever found him a dull companion. Indeed he had difficulty in controlling his effervescent sense of humour and often ran the risk of being thought frivolous by solemn-minded folk. Starting with *Arms and the Man* (1894), he embarked on a series of plays written in popular style, but his imitation of conventional dramatic structures was highly individual. It might seem that Shaw was actually sending up the kind of play he had apparently set out to write. The question of whether he has ended by mocking a familiar type of play may even be asked of *The Devil's Disciple*.

Neither *Arms and the Man* nor *Candida* (both written in 1894) concentrates on glaring social evils or seems to have any political aim. They are written more to be entertaining than disturbing. *Arms and the Man* attacks the glorification of war, but by the methods of ridicule, using the techniques of farcical comedy to make the audience laugh often and laugh long. *Candida* quietly raises questions about the Victorians' idealization of the home and the influence of the perfect wife and mother, while passing itself off as a conventional, slightly sentimental celebration of these very ideals. When he came to publish the collection of his plays in 1898, Shaw gave it the title of *Plays Pleasant and Unpleasant*.

The first of the two volumes contained the 'unpleasant' plays, including *Widowers' Houses* and *Mrs Warren's Profession*. *Arms and the Man* and *Candida* were classified as 'pleasant' and published in the second volume.

Continuing difficulties

Arms and the Man was produced in London in 1894, in a limited season of new plays specially financed by Miss Annie Horniman, who was to become the patron of the Irish National Theatre in Dublin. Such sponsorship was necessary because ordinary theatre managers were reluctant to put on any morally or artistically serious new plays, and they would not take a risk with Shaw's. This was his reason for publishing them with specially written descriptions of settings and characters that made it possible to read them as if they were novels. He added prefaces to make them more saleable in book form to the general public and to distinguish them further from acting editions of plays, normally published simply for those who wanted to perform them. The books were, indeed, a success. However, it now became customary for people to admit the cleverness of his writing, while arguing that, of course, these were not really plays at all and would not work on the stage. As far as most of them were concerned, the opinion was not disproved until Shaw's young friend, Granville Barker, took the Court Theatre in London's Sloane Square from 1904 to 1907, and demonstrated beyond dispute just how theatrically effective they were. After this, Shaw steadily became the best-known and most frequently performed modern British playwright throughout the world. He wrote many more plays in the course of his long life, the best-known being *Man and Superman*, *Major Barbara*, *Pygmalion* and *Saint Joan*. Doubts about his work are now more often expressed by literary critics reading the texts rather than by experienced directors, actors and theatre managers.

The Devil's Disciple was the only one of Shaw's plays to achieve a successful run in the commercial theatre before Granville Barker's enterprise. This may be explained in part by the fact that it is an American play in its setting and story; for the run took place in New York in 1897, with the romantic actor, Richard Mansfield, playing the part of Dick Dudgeon. The success was an encouragement to others, particularly to the distinguished British actor-manager, (Sir) Johnston Forbes Robertson, who played Dick in England in 1900.

Shaw as a man of the theatre

Shaw himself was thoroughly at home in the theatre, not only as a critic sitting in the stalls on first nights. He had something of an actor's personality and clearly enjoyed performing before an audience. He belonged to amateur play-reading societies and took part with Karl Marx's daughter, Eleanor, in an amateur performance of Ibsen's *A Doll's House*. It was his custom to try out his plays by reading them to a select audience before he finalized the text, and there is plentiful testimony to the effectiveness of his reading. He had a wide acquaintance with the work of actors and actresses of his day and liked to choose the casts for his own plays. Whenever possible, he would take a hand in the production, directing some rehearsals himself or, at the very least, watching rehearsals and sending precise notes of advice and criticism to the players. The style of acting he favoured for his plays, and that he seems to have had in mind as he wrote them, was what we would call 'stagey', rather broad and exaggerated, a style used by the older classic actors of his day and that had been developed in huge theatres, where many of the audience were a considerable distance from the stage. He was not what is often called a 'naturalistic' dramatist, trying to make his plays look and sound as if they were slices of actual everyday life, though he was certainly concerned with truthfulness to human nature. Indeed he advised that his plays ought to be presented rather as if they were Italian opera: going for big effects, not being afraid of strong emotional expression and the eloquence of the dialogue, especially noticeable in the long speeches which he wanted spoken with such skill as opera singers need to apply to their arias. (This type of rhetorical speech was to be fully developed in the plays of his middle period as a dramatist. Shaw is only beginning to move towards it in *The Devil's Disciple*.) He had learnt at first hand, as a street-corner speaker for socialism as well as on many indoor public platforms, what a hold an accomplished orator could get on a crowd and, also, what excitement could be generated by the cut-and-thrust of impassioned public debate on crucial issues. The blend of argument with emotional excitement, introduced into stage plays, became one of his main contributions as a dramatist.

Plays for Puritans

The Devil's Disciple, in its turn, was published in 1901 as an item in the second collection of Shaw's drama, entitled *Three Plays for Puritans*. Its companion plays were *Captain Brassbound's Conversion*, also a melodrama, and *Caesar and Cleopatra*, which presents Shaw's view of one of the great military leaders of history. In the first part of the Preface to this collection, printed in this book on pages 1–15, he indicates the sense in which these are plays 'for puritans', written by a man who shares their rejection of 'the drama of romance and sensuality' (page 4). The Preface is out-of-date in various ways: the theatre it describes is not the theatre of today, and attitudes it regards as commonplace are quite rare now; not least, a present-day writer would be unlikely to write about sex and 'voluptuousness' just as Shaw does, leaving us somewhat unconvinced by his protests that he is not prudish. His complaint that, as a theatre critic, he grew very tired of the quantity of plays that had little to offer but the most conventional 'love interest' is easier to accept and understand. In view of this, each of the three plays in the collection can be seen as raising the possibility of 'love interest' (rather late in *Captain Brassbound's Conversion*), only to set it aside to make way for another theme. Other 'romantic' notions are brought into question by characters with a commonsense, practical approach to the world. There is little doubt that the romantic elements in these plays, like their exotic settings (the Sahara Desert, eighteenth-century America during a war, and Ancient Egypt), contribute to the pleasure they may give. Yet this pleasure is enhanced by something unconventional in the treatment that disperses the dreamy languor, or mere senti-mentality, of 'romance'. There is more fun in them than in the type of play Shaw objected to.

He distrusted the kind of puritanism that had no sense of fun and that even disapproved of it. This is the kind of puritanism represented by Mrs Dudgeon and Dick's aunts and uncles, in *The Devil's Disciple*. In *Captain Brassbound's Conversion*, Shaw attacks a rigid attachment to justice, without the mercy of humour, as a puritan attitude. Traditionally, puritans have disapproved of the theatre and even wanted to close it. Shaw was no puritan in choosing to write for it, while seeing so clearly that it is a place for fun, for play, offering make-believe, not reality, as he indicates in referring to 'the play of ideas', adding '—and the drama can never be anything more—' (Preface, page 3).

Playing with ideas is something very different from preaching or formal instruction. It involves freely trying them out and as readily tossing them aside. So Shaw's plays give us ideas to think about, even if we cannot always take seriously the form in which they are presented. They do not lay down the law in the form of absolute conclusions. He also takes full advantage of the dramatic form to present different, often opposed views through different characters, making us see round the matters under discussion, making us recognize that there is something valid to be said on each side, and that there are often more than two sides to a question. Although Richard Dudgeon has always been the star part in *The Devil's Disciple*, Anthony Ander-son draws attention away from him and even prompts a re-consideration of Dick's character: whether he is more a hero, or a fool. The question, seeing the two possibilities, is more important than the answer.

A melodrama

When Shaw wrote *The Devil's Disciple*, it was the theatre alone that supplied the kind of entertainment people get from the cinema or television today. Certain theatres specialized in one particular type of play: at the Adelphi Theatre, London, under the management of William Terriss (1848–1897), who was also the star actor in his own theatre, the public could expect to see melodramas. These were plays that reflected the tastes and values of the lower middle class, the class of clerks and shop girls, though they were often popular with a wider social range. The hero and heroine of a melodrama were commonly poor, but honest. The trials and adventures they underwent, which made up the typical plot of melodrama, were usually brought about by the villainous plans or deceptive wiles of upper-class characters. Even if the plot did not follow these lines, it aimed at a thrilling, exciting effect, and it was not difficult to distinguish between the innocent and virtuous characters and their sinister, often more sophisticated and guiltily experienced persecutors. The term, 'melodrama', refers to the use of music to heighten the dramatic effect of the play: characters had their own 'signature tunes', which enhanced the impression they gave of being, perhaps, sweet and sympathetic, straightforward and brave, or terrifying, or untrustworthy; and the mood of particular scenes was intensified by the playing of appropriate music. Indeed, the piano accompaniment to early silent films, many of which were melodramas, was intermediate between stage melodrama and the often very subtle use of background music in modern films.

William Terriss approached Shaw early in 1896 with the suggestion that they should write a melodrama together.

Although he turned down the proposal at that time and in that form, the idea lingered in Shaw's mind. He was familiar with the plots and technique of melodrama from his early days of theatre-going in Dublin as well as from his more recent professional experience as theatre critic for *The Saturday Review* in London. So he set to work writing *The Devil's Disciple* as a play for Terriss, though the latter's sudden death in 1897 (he was murdered outside his stage door) meant that the finished play went to other managements. In a letter of 3 May 1899, to Mrs Richard Mansfield, wife of the first actor to play Dick Dudgeon, Shaw declared:

> *The Devil's Disciple* is a melodrama, made up of all the stale Adelphi tricks – the reading of the will, the heroic sacrifice, the court martial, the execution, the reprieve at the last moment. Anybody could make a play that way.

This disparaging account of it is far from being a complete description of *The Devil's Disciple*, but it certainly testifies to the dramatic models Shaw had in mind as he wrote, and to his conscious use of well-known conventions, or clichés, of plot.

Plays about evil

Melodramas are essentially thrillers, though, like the Hammer Company's horror films, they often contain a comic character or two. They are concerned with manifestations of evil or entirely mundane wicked deeds. *The Devil's Disciple*, as the title of a play, arouses expectations of the supernatural, a programme that may include the worship of evil in some form of black mass, the calling-up of spirits from hell, perhaps the selling or dedication of a soul to the devil: some hocus pocus designed to have us delightfully shrieking at calculated shock after shock. If this is the kind of entertainment we are after, Shaw's play will disappoint us; we must find different qualities in it to enjoy. Yet the title is not irrelevant. Dick Dudgeon claims it for himself (page 45):

> ... I knew from the first that the Devil was my natural master and captain and friend ... I promised him my soul ... From this day this house is his home ...

The rebel as villain or hero

The very fact that he talks like this is enough to explain the way in which others regard him. There is something daring, to say the least, even in a verbal rejection of God and of what society generally considers to be good: the sin of blasphemy is particularly frightening to timid souls. Very little is said about other ways in which Dick is wicked. We hear about some involvement with smugglers and gipsies, but there is no suggestion that he risks arrest for any crime, when he arrives for the reading of his father's Will. He has not murdered anyone, or kidnapped anyone. When the minister returns to find his wife lying unconscious on the floor, we realize that Dick might appear to have assaulted or raped her; but Anderson, though worried, does not voice a suspicion of this. Without comment, Shaw hints at the kind of wicked deed committed by typical villains in melodrama, when we know that Dick has not behaved this way at all. It could be said that appearances are against him – as when the soldiers find him at table with Judith (page 57).

The twentieth century affords us many examples of how individuals, or minority groups, with very little power, can frighten those who belong to the majority and have the force of custom, money and the law behind them. These 'villains' have managed to frighten 'respectable' people without having to do anything criminal or violent. An unconventional appearance may be enough, perhaps the brutal associations of chains and black leather jackets; and there is a curious power in names: it is not a far cry from the 'devil's disciple' to the 'hell's angel'; and Dick Dudgeon would certainly have understood and respected the motives of those who chose for themselves such names as 'Rotten' and 'Vicious'. A solitary chalk-white face and mohican hairstyle in the street at night was not just freaky before it became fashionable. To older people, set in their ways, it posed such questions as 'What is the world coming to?' 'Is civilization crumbling?' 'Why do they hate us?' or 'Where have we gone wrong?' It advertized the alien, the barbaric, without respect for accepted, traditional values. It took courage and daring to shed the clothing of the herd and stand alone and exposed like some exotic bird or highly coloured poisonous flower that the fearful are tempted to destroy. Above all, such monstrous appearances declare: 'We don't want your approval; we don't want you to like us; we are not amiable and affectionate like spaniels; it is not safe to be near us, we are unpredictable; the world is not yours alone: we'll see to it that you don't go on thinking it a comfortable place in which you are at home.' What the rebel has done is assume the posture of attack, thus altering the psychological situation. He or she has taken the initiative away from those who have assumed it lies naturally with them. They have felt secure and unchallengeable; now they are on the defensive.

Growing up and rejecting God

Rejecting their parents is a necessary part of growing up for very many human beings. They do not find themselves until they have gone through this phase. Some are never able to feel entirely secure from the pressure of their elders and have to keep fighting it off, reacting negatively against it, for the rest of their lives. A grand, mythic version of this refusal to go on submitting to the law laid down by someone else is the rebellion of the archangel Lucifer, thereafter known as Satan, against God. The story is part of Christian tradition, made more familiar through John Milton's account in *Paradise Lost* (published in 1667), the greatest literary product of the English puritan revolution of the seventeenth century. William Blake (1757–1827), whom Shaw mentions in his Preface to *The Devil's Disciple* (page 19), illustrated and printed his own magnificent edition of *Paradise Lost* and was so struck by the heroic treatment of Satan that he declared Milton was 'of the devil's party without knowing it'. The moral code, values and standards of 'the devil's party' are what Shaw calls 'diabolonian ethics', which are a radical challenge to the beliefs and standards generally upheld in society. It is interesting to note that Blake invented the name 'Nobodaddy' for the false idea of God many of his contemporaries seemed to worship.

The play in relation to history

Shaw's Note on General Burgoyne (see page 97) refers to the only specific historical source he used when writing *The Devil's Disciple*, but his play reflects certain facts on which historians have agreed. These are: that there was a plan for General Burgoyne and his troops to proceed from Canada (Quebec) into the valley of the River Hudson in order to separate New England from the rest of the American colonies, and that he was to be joined at Albany by General Howe and his army in August 1777. Burgoyne reached Albany and scored a victory over an uneasy combination of New England troops and others from New York, but blunders in the management of the war from London had allowed Howe to move in another direction entirely – by sea to Chesapeake Bay. Burgoyne's army moved slowly on the west side of the Hudson, hampered by its baggage and running perilously short of supplies; they attacked the Americans on 19 September and again on 7 October, winning the first battle, but being badly defeated in the second in the absence of help from General Clinton and his forces in New York. Burgoyne found himself surrounded, asked for a truce, and surrendered to General Gates at Saratoga on 17 October.

Timothy Dudgeon's Will is dated 'this twenty-fourth day of September one thousand seven hundred and seventy seven'. The significance of the year was emphasized by Shaw when he was altering the play for the cinema screen and chose to start with George Washington signing the American colonies' Declaration of Independence in 1776 (see Appendix to this Introduction, pages xlix–l). The events of the play are supposed to fit into two imaginary days and Shaw has made certain adjustments in the historical facts to simplify the story: he has shifted Burgoyne's arrival at Albany forward more than a month to late September; he does not correct the false impression that Howe, not Clinton, is at New York; he allows Burgoyne to realize that the whole plan of campaign has gone wrong and to foresee that he will have to surrender at Saratoga (page 87). Furthermore, Burgoyne's reflection that the rebels may have found themselves a leader in Anderson ignores the fact that George Washington was the Americans' acknowledged commander-in-chief and Benedict Arnold their successful general in the field.

Evidently, dramatizing the facts of history was not Shaw's aim: either he was careless of them and relied on the ignorance of his audience to help him preserve the illusion of historical accuracy; or he deliberately altered them to suit some other purpose. He is certainly not addressing his play to an audience of specialist historians, but to men and women with a smattering of historical knowledge, perhaps half-remembered from school-days, and for whom world history is mainly a popular source book of interesting stories.

Personal and public stories

The question remains: was Shaw simply exploiting the American War setting for its picturesque and romantic values, or was he seriously concerned to give an interpretation of that historical episode, some meaning or lesson to be learned from the War of Independence, that he wanted his play to put across? It is worth remarking that he presents public scenes as well as domestic scenes, keeping a rough balance between the private lives of his characters and the political history in which they are caught up. Both the story of Dick Dudgeon and the setting near a frontier during the War of Independence were present from the beginning, in Shaw's first draft of the play, before he had decided on the lines his plot was finally to take, or on the exact use he was going to make of the historical figure of General Burgoyne. So great an event as the emergence of the USA as an independent power might well make the personal story seem trivial, unless the two were presented as closely linked in some serious way. Someone without any previous knowledge of how the Americans won the war might be forgiven for assuming from the play that Anthony Anderson's rescue of Dick Dudgeon was a decisive incident in the struggle. By having Burgoyne speculate, 'Suppose the colonists find a leader! Suppose the news from Springtown should turn out to mean that they have already found a leader!' (page 75), Shaw invites us to wonder whether Anderson, converted from minister to soldier, might not be that leader. Those who know their American history will realize that this is nonsense. They will also notice that Richard is outspoken in his defiance of King George and his troops, and that he is identified by Anderson as 'that American citizen', as the order for his release is given (page 93). At this moment, Dick represents the colonists in general, and his liberation prefigures theirs. We may be justified in seeing a parallel between his personal rebellion against the religious community of his elders and the Americans' successful rebellion against English rule. It is like an unstressed hint that the feelings and motives that shape individual lives may also be the basis for the large-scale changes of world history: neither is less of a *human* phenomenon than the other.

The structure of the play: plot and action

In the shaping of his play, Shaw has interwoven two plots: one involving the reform of Dick Dudgeon and the other presenting the progress of the war and the relations between King George's troops and the New Englanders. The chief incidents of the first of these plots are presented directly on stage; the second seems to take place largely offstage, but is reflected in the comments, fears and expectations of the characters on stage; and what happens in the war – the taking and re-taking of towns, the movements of troops and their condition – impinges on the first plot and affects its development. The forward thrust of events, what may be called the dramatic action, is clearly marked in the scenes Shaw has chosen to present. In Act I, the news is given of the hanging of Peter Dudgeon by troops thirty miles away, but the main business of the scene is Timothy Dudgeon's Will, which changes Dick from a social outcast to a man of property; in Act II, he is tamed, his manners are further civilized by the treatment he gets in Anderson's house, until his new respect for the minister and humane (civilized) concern for Judith are capped by the help he freely gives them, through his acceptance of the soldiers' mistake. What is happening in the war, the stuff of the second plot, creates the situation in which Dick first shows loyalty to another man and fellow-citizen. In the scenes of Act III, the two plots march together, as Burgoyne's attention is divided between what is happening elsewhere in the war and the stage events of Dick's trial and preparations for his execution.

Dick's spiritual development is part of the dramatic action and it can be traced in his behaviour as Act III proceeds. Shaw has moved gradually from showing the change in Dick's social status to what seems a profound inner change – unless we interpret this as a revelation of what has been his true character all along. Judith Anderson's shifting attitudes to Richard and to her husband can likewise be traced from Act I to the end of the play, and make a complication in the personal plot.

Hero or fool?

The word 'hero' can be used to describe either a person who acts bravely or a character in a play (or novel) who attracts and holds the audience's attention, admiration and sympathy. However many others are on stage, the hero is the one the audience is most interested in. In this sense, Dick plays the hero in Act I: though his relations may not admire him, they cannot ignore him. He dominates them by his behaviour, and the audience watching the play notices how the advantage stays with him as he vexes or embarrasses one after another of the group in Mrs Dudgeon's room. The lawyer and the minister let him get on with it, and Essie's presence and response to him allow him to show a generous, easy kindness, of which the others seem rather short. We have probably all imagined ourselves controlling a difficult situation in that way, perhaps thinking after the event what we might have said to put others down. Richard is undoubtedly more comfortable in this defiant position than he would be slinking around, feeling ashamed and humiliated while everyone scolded him – if he behaved rather as Essie does.

When he is arrested, stands trial and waits to be executed as Anthony Anderson, he is a different kind of hero: strong in his silence and resoluteness, not aggressive now. His words and behaviour at the trial make him seem superior to others – and equal to the aristocratic Burgoyne – in the control of his emotions and his general air of philosophic indifference to whatever may befall: a man superior to circumstances. It is when Anderson returns to release Dick that the latter's passivity becomes obvious: he has maintained the pose of a self-sacrificing hero (not drawing back when death is upon him), while Anderson has not bothered about what people think of him, but has got on with the job of organizing the Springtown rebels. Now Anderson looks like the practical man and Dick Dudgeon like a romantic, perhaps even a self-dramatizing romantic.

The contrast between the two bears some resemblance to that between the chief male characters in Shaw's earlier play, *Arms and the Man*: the experienced mercenary soldier, Bluntschli, who has no illusions about war and regards careful planning and the avoidance of unnecessary risks as essential to victory, and the highborn officer, Sergius, who charges to battle on horseback, well ahead of his men, waving his sword in the face of the enemy's cannon – and only escapes because they cannot believe their eyes. In *The Devil's Disciple*, Shaw sets a third type alongside the romantic and the practical realist: this is the cynic, the man who thinks worse of others than of himself, the type General Burgoyne represents. Shaw may not have made up his mind finally about Burgoyne. He drew attention to the character's callous cruelty, in a letter to Mrs Richard Mansfield, and this suggests that he may have intended him to be a variation on the conventional aristocratic villain of melodrama, the true villain, after Dick has been revealed as a sham villain. Then in the last scene he lets Burgoyne declare himself 'humane enough to be glad' of his defeat (page 94), which has also meant the freeing of Richard. Shaw's disbelief in villains, in thoroughly evil people, probably shows in this inconsistency.

Heroic self-sacrifice

Dick's readiness to die in another man's place is undeniably heroic. It is so extreme as to be almost unbelievable: the kind of heroism that would surprise us greatly in ordinary life. It would have seemed quite natural if he had protested to the soldiers immediately that they were making a mistake or, once arrested, if he had done everything in his power to prove his true identity. Such selfless bravery is romantic, the kind of thing we come across in stories and legends, or the stuff of daydreams. Why Dick should behave this way has been much discussed.

Charles Dickens's novel *A Tale of Two Cities* contains a similar episode, very important in the plot: Sidney Carton, an English lawyer, goes to the guillotine in place of the French aristocrat, Charles Darnay, whom he closely resembles. Carton, who dies, whereas Dick is rescued at the last moment, is motivated chiefly by his secret love for Darnay's wife, Lucy, though he also feels self-disgust at the way he has wasted his own life. Dickens himself collaborated with a successful playwright, Tom Taylor, in turning this book into a melodrama in 1860. It was the first of more than half a dozen plays based on the same story to be written in the remainder of the nineteenth century. The most famous of them today is Freeman Wills's *The Only Way*, written after *The Devil's Disciple*, but before its first London production. Martin Harvey (later Sir John Martin-Harvey), an actor in the romantic style, had his greatest success playing Sidney Carton in this play and made a great impression with the speech he – rather quietly and unrhetorically – delivered from the scaffold: 'It is a far, far better thing I do than I have ever done . . .'

Yet another play, *The Dead Heart* by Watts Phillips, acted at the Lyceum Theatre by the great Henry Irving in 1889 and known to Shaw, makes use of the same plot element of a man who dies by the guillotine in another's place, because of his love for a woman. So Shaw was deliberately presenting a story of a well-known and popular type, running the risk that audiences would not notice the differences he was introducing; indeed they might not want to notice them, preferring the usual version. His Preface tells (pages 21–22) of how the wish to keep a romantic love interest at the centre of the play influenced a critic and the actors performing *The Devil's Disciple*. No one seems to have been troubled by the fact that Shaw did not transfer Sidney Carton's other motive – remorse over a wasted life – to Dick Dudgeon, either. He could well have done so, if he had wished to show Dick as a repentant, converted character, in the second half of the play. Perhaps his view of rebellion as healthy and useful meant that the devil's disciple had nothing to repent of, in his author's opinion. Certainly, having no obvious personal motives for his act makes Dick's behaviour more like that of the devil's traditional antagonist, Christ, the supreme example of dying that others may live, whoever they are.

Shaw and religion

In his Preface (page 19), Shaw acknowledges the influence of

Charles Dickens's portrayal of Mrs Clennam, in *Little Dorrit*, on his own conception of Mrs Dudgeon. *Little Dorrit* is set in Victorian England, and Mrs Clennam embodies the negative, repressive quality of Victorian puritanism, which insisted on what should NOT be done to the exclusion of positive values and allowed no freedom to natural energy and high spirits – least of all on Sundays. As a Victorian himself, Shaw was familiar with this attitude, and its survival into the time when he wrote *The Devil's Disciple* gave him one of his chief themes for the play. The historical puritanism of Mrs Dudgeon mattered to him because it was alive in his own day, and it matters today because killjoy attitudes and people who love nothing better than to complain are still about; indeed very many of us can slip into moods of that sort only too easily.

Shaw's family does not seem to have been puritanical in the Dudgeon way, except in his mother's attutude to his father's drinking and fecklessness, which gave her a great deal to put up with. There was a good deal of joking about religion among his father and uncles, and the adolescent Bernard Shaw was proud to be an atheist, at a time when virtually everybody believed in God. Though he consistently protested, in later life, that he was a religious man and interested in the subject of religion above all others, he never used these terms in a narrow, orthodox sense and never came to believe in an all-powerful God, above and outside humanity and nature; he considered that men and women had to look within themselves to find spiritual values and, perhaps, an idea or principle that they might choose to call God. The idea he was to adopt for himself he called Creative Evolution, indicating that his was a religion that did not conflict with science and the evolutionary theory of nineteenth-century scientists in particular, though he did not agree with Darwin's version of this theory. Some of his later plays, notably *Man and Superman* (1903–5) and *Back to Methuselah* (1921), present the notion of Creative Evolution in a light-hearted way. *The Devil's Disciple* does not go further than showing that true religion is not what a man or woman claims to believe, but the deep-seated convictions that actually determine what they do: convictions they may not think of as religious at all.

His familiarity with the Bible

In the course of his own spiritual search, Shaw studied the Bible more thoroughly than most professing Christians do. He knew much of it by heart and could quote freely from it. He praised it as a great work of literature, full of human interest, and his own style of writing was much influenced by the rhythms, cadences, turns of phrase, images, and even the system of punctuation used in the King James version (the translation of the Bible made and authorized for use in churches in the early seventeenth century and kept in nearly every home well into this present century). The biblical language in *The Devil's Disciple* is used in a particularly appropriate way. As it comes from the mouths of the characters, it helps create a sense of the historical period and the community to which they belong.

The settings and dramatic rhythm

The play unfolds through six scenes, taking place within five different settings. Shaw has not numbered the separate scenes within the three Acts, perhaps because he wanted the breaks within the Acts to be as brief as possible. The whole of Act I is a single, continuous scene set in Mrs Dudgeon's living room. Act II similarly keeps to a single setting, the contrasting domestic interior of the Andersons' house; but it is divided into two scenes, marked off from each other by different lighting, which reinforces a change of mood as well as indicating that some time has passed. Act III consists of three scenes in three different settings. Shaw indicated in his manuscript draft of the play that the first of these, in the waiting room, should be a 'front scene', allowing for the stage set for the Court Room to be in position, but concealed, before the Act starts. Thus Judith can move straight from one scene into the next, as though going immediately out of one room into a second. The third scene has a different location again, in the open air of the Websterbridge Market Place. Again the characters are supposed to move immediately, though over a somewhat greater distance, from one scene into the next. Indeed the Market Place could be represented in another front scene with a scaffold put in position while the lights were down; and the limiting of the stage space could even give the impression of a larger crowd, in a greater crush round the prisoner and his guards, as though passing in from a much wider area, invisible to the audience. When the play was to be produced in French, at the Odéon in Paris, in 1926, Shaw sent sketches for the sets and urged that the *three* sets for Act III should be in place before the rise of the curtain, the Market Place being furthest upstage. He wanted no more than 45 seconds to elapse between scene 2 and scene 3.

The last two scenes are obviously more colourful and spectacular than the domestic scenes of Acts I and II. Even in this visual way, Shaw has made sure that the later part of his play will be more exciting than what has gone before. Variety is provided through further contrasts: as between the red coats of the soldiers in Act III and the dark clothes of the puritans in Act I, or between the intimacy of the scene when Richard is alone with Judith in Act II, and the final crowd scene with the bands playing. Whether the audience consciously notices it or not, Shaw's stagecraft conveys an impression of the play opening up, as Dick moves from his unhappy involvement with his family and his personal bitterness into the role he finds in the community at large, and from being almost an outlaw to the public recognition expressed when the townspeople lift him on their shoulders. The dramatist has recognized that part of his task is to give his play a satisfying overall rhythm, and the sequence and location of his scenes contributes to this, as well as giving his story shape and logical sense.

Keeping an eye on the time

Shaw mentions that there is a pendulum clock hanging on the wall in Mrs Dudgeon's room. His description of it, with its 'white wooden dial', implies that he wants it to be noticed, and it is worth considering what would be the effect in performance of hearing its tick and even, perhaps, seeing it mark the time. Act I moves from phase to phase in an unbroken series, bringing in quite a large number of characters: we see Mrs Dudgeon with Essie, then Christy arrives with startling news, followed by Anderson and, quickly, by the visitors – singly or in groups – come to hear the Will of the man whose death has only just been reported; and so the action continues, until Mrs Dudgeon departs from the house that, at the start, had seemed her secure home, and Essie is left with hopes of a very different future under Dick's protection. To get the effect of interest and excitement steadily building up, through the concentration of developments into such a limited period of actual time, a reader needs to try and go through the Act without pausing.

A similar control ensures the generally rapid sequence of events throughout the rest of the play and introduces a sense of urgency into what might otherwise seem rather static passages (as in exchanges of dialogue at the trial). Pointed references to the time are made at intervals in Act II and Act III, and the town clock races Dick towards his death. By calling Burgoyne's elaborate watch a *chronometer* (page 92) – an instrument to measure time – Shaw gives another clue to the technique he is using to make his play tense and thrilling. In Act III, his non-realistic speeding up of events is complicated by the way in which he relates what is happening on stage to what is supposed to be simultaneous offstage action: Anderson's ride to Springtown, the events that he sets in train there, and his return ride to Websterbridge. (The fact that the two places are thirty miles apart is mentioned casually by Mrs Dudgeon in Act I, and Timothy Dudgeon's reported death at Nevinstown – between the two – may have the effect of making the distance seem greater.) Another, slightly different pressure of offstage events comes from Burgoyne's preoccupation with news of troop movements and delays.

The finale

Near the end of the play, Shaw uses a trick of dramatic fore-shortening to create an impression that Anderson's rousing of Springtown and his bringing to terms of Burgoyne have decided the issue of the war: America has won its freedom and the British have to admit defeat. Max Beerbohm (1872–1956), reviewing the short-lived London production of *The Devil's Disciple* at Kennington in 1900, commented that the play 'suddenly tumbled into wild frivolity' at the end. He did not reflect on the means Shaw used to create such a mood, beyond simple reliance on the lifting of tension when the threat of imminent death is withdrawn. The reader in the study can get further by examining the text alertly (page 93):

> ANDERSON ... Thank God, I was in time!
> BURGOYNE (... *watch in hand*) Ample time, sir. ... I should never dream of hanging any gentleman by an American clock.
> ANDERSON Yes: we are some minutes ahead of you already, General. Now tell them to take the rope from the neck of that American citizen.

The dialogue has turned into a fabric of little jokes, and the jokes about time are turned in Anderson's last speech here into a deliberately engineered effect of anachronism: cheap American clocks of no great accuracy flooded the English market in the late nineteenth century, not in the previous century, and the words, 'we are some minutes ahead of you already' would not have made sense in 1777; indeed the setting up of international time zones was topical when the play was new. Rather like the process of waking out of a dream, the play is bringing us back from a fantasy of being in the eighteenth century to the reality of our own times (or, strictly speaking, of the time when Shaw wrote the play and the first audiences saw it). A few lines later we have:

> BURGOYNE *(to Swindon)* You look disappointed, Major Swin-
>   don.
> SWINDON You look defeated, General Burgoyne.

The pattern of words is obviously artificial and, though it is not protracted, it resembles the way in which comedians performing a double act echo each other and cap each other's lines amusingly. A historical foreshortening is happening here, too, in this labelling of Burgoyne, before the event, as the defeated English general. The jokes and anachronisms continue:

> without a Conquest you cannot have an aristocracy . . .

> Take it quietly, Major Swindon: your friend the British soldier can stand up to anything except the British War Office.

Shaw might have retorted that this last joke is always topical, even when the War Office is called the Ministry of Defence. Still, the effect depends on our sense of two different periods and recognition that people of the twentieth century and inhabitants of the eighteenth century can smile at each other sympathetically over a common experience. Other lines in the last few moments of the play have the effect of neatly summing up, or rounding off events, as life never is rounded off:

> RICHARD . . . I have behaved like a fool.
> JUDITH Like a hero.

Again, in Anderson's summary: 'It takes all sorts to make a world – saints as well as soldiers.' Shaw's provisions for a crowded

xl

stage, bands playing rousing music, and the cheering of Dick, make as much of a grand finale – the thoroughly theatrical, triumphant end of the show – as he wants. Whatever they have learned in the course of the play, the audience should leave the theatre with the sense of having been entertained. It is worth noting that the antagonists in the play go off to have lunch together.

Costume and disguise

Costume has always been a simple means of identifying characters on stage: a king, a cardinal, a clown can be recognized as such before the actor has much chance to suggest individual qualities, and a lovely dress will do more than actual features to suggest a pretty woman. In *The Devil's Disciple*, the soldiers are immediately recognizable by their costume. So is the clergyman – until he leaves his black coat at home and Dick Dudgeon puts it on, causing prolonged confusion. This is not what is usually meant as disguise, though Dick certainly begins to impersonate a minister as soon as he speaks to the Sergeant: 'thank you kindly for the apology' is not the style of talk we have heard from him before. Just like an actor, he has put on a manner appropriate to the costume. The coat and the manner prompt respect and politeness from the Sergeant, for they are signs of spiritual authority and social position. More remarkably, putting them on denotes an actual change in Richard's character: from being an irreverent blasphemer he has become an ideal Christian, ready to give his life for a fellow human being. In fact, Shaw does not merely use the coat as a sign of the office or profession of clergyman, he uses it as an outward sign or symbol of the true character that Richard's defiant bravado has been hiding.

When Anderson returns in Act III, he declares, 'you may keep my coat and I'll keep yours', for he has discovered that another way of life suits him better than a clergyman's. What is involved is more than a change of profession: he has discovered the truth about his own nature, that he is a man of action, energetic and eager to struggle in the world, rather than a man of prayer and quiet thought, affecting the world indirectly through his influence as a counsellor and preacher over the consciences of others.

Shaw prepared the way for this dramatic use of costume by his dressing of the characters in Act I. There are individual differences between the Dudgeon relatives, but their respectable mourning garb gives them an identity as a group that is stronger than their personal identity, and the dark colours they wear have a severe, rather depressing effect that directly expresses a quality in their religion. Richard's careless dress indicates his rejection of the group's conventions and emphasizes his detachment from the formal proceedings and his attitude to established order generally. Yet the most surprising costume is worn by the lawyer, Mr Hawkins. Shaw might well have given him a decently dark suit, a variation on the clergyman's. Instead, though he is present as part of his professional duties, he is dressed 'in brown riding gaiters and yellow breeches' like a squire or gentleman farmer. It draws attention to the character, as the touch of colour brightens up the scene. This lawyer is not limited by his profession, a mere functionary sinking into the background. His dress turns him into an individual worth watching carefully, a disturbing element in the scene. (It is also a costume implying a special position that puts him out of range of the criticism of people like the Dudgeons.) Here is an early lesson in not judging on appearances and not taking people at face value. Shaw's ultimate suggestion that costume needs to be thought about seriously comes in Judith's challenging words to Burgoyne (page 80):

> Is it nothing to you whether you are a murderer or not, if only you murder in a red coat?

They should ensure that we look carefully at the Chaplain, wearing his white surplice, in the last scene of the play; for costume may be used by men and women as something to hide behind, pleading, 'It's part of the job', or 'I'm only carrying out orders', or even 'It's not my job, not my responsibility'. It is worth considering the most elaborate of the settings, the Court Room, as a room dressed up.

Shaw uses the ordinary trappings of stage performance to suggest meanings, but these meanings are not fixed and constant. They have to be judged afresh in each particular context; and it is not always ideas that are suggested. Colour, like music, has an emotional effect on us. Red is an exciting colour that may be associated with battle and bloodshed, or with life, vigour and high spirits. White has traditional associations with inno-cence. In the final scene, the mass uniforms of the soldiers make a solid background to the single, lonely figure of Dick, whose white shirt makes him look more vulnerable and so enlists our sympathies more strongly on his side. When events take their sudden happy turn, and the soldiers break out of formation, the red of their tunics enhances the celebratory mood of the end of the play.

The character scheme

In a letter to the leading actress of the time, Ellen Terry, Bernard Shaw commented on *The Devil's Disciple* as he was writing it:

> Burgoyne is a gentleman ... It is not enough, for the instruc-tion of this generation, that Richard should be superior to religion and morality as typified by his mother and his home, or to love as typified by Judith. He must also be superior to gentility – that is to the whole ideal of modern society.

The remark makes it clear that Shaw was not just imagining people in whom he might interest his audiences and giving actors lines to speak and other suggestions that would help bring the characters to life on the stage. His story is not only a story, but shaped and presented to guide our thinking and convey, or suggest, certain meanings. The play does not necessarily conform exactly to the meanings sketched in the letter. Certainly that definiteness, those hard, clear lines are likely to have been modified, or blurred, in the writing process. Equally certainly, other meanings are implied in the play, when it is approached from other points of view. Taken with these reservations, the hint is valuable: here is an indication that each of the three Acts of the play brings in a different subject and that Shaw, in choosing characters for his play, wanted to associate them with particular subjects or values. In recognizing Mrs Dudgeon, Judith, or Burgoyne, we are not just recognizing their individual features and idiosyncrasies; we identify each of them with a general attitude to life and with something abstract like morality, love, the code of a gentleman.

This goes some way to explain why the new character of Burgoyne has been brought into Act III, rather late for a major character to appear. Similarly, it gives a reason for the disappearance of Mrs Dudgeon with the end of Act I: Shaw was passing from an examination of puritanism to fresh topics, and so this character had served its purpose. Being more interested in the play as a whole than in any single figure, and as her presence would certainly not add to the gaiety of the ending, he kills her off without a second thought, as soon as he has used her as an excuse to remove Anderson from the stage in Act II.

Anderson is the other major character not mentioned in the letter at that point. As the business with the coats shows, Shaw sets Richard Dudgeon alongside Anderson for consideration and comparison at least as deliberately as he is set beside the others. The difference is that there is no question of superiority here; Anderson is in no way put down by Dick. His words in the last Act suggest that they have permanently changed places with each other (page 94):

This foolish young man ... boasted himself the Devil's Disciple; but ... he found that it was his destiny to suffer and be faithful to the death. I thought myself a decent minister of the gospel of peace; but ... I found that it was my destiny to be a

> man of action ... So I am starting life at fifty as Captain
> Anthony Anderson of the Springtown militia; and the Devil's
> Disciple here will start presently as the Reverend Richard
> Dudgeon, and wag his pow in my old pulpit ...

This is very schematic. Only the use of the humorous expression,
'wag his pow', allows us to interpret Anderson's whole comment
as humorous in tone, teasing Dick rather than seriously an-
nouncing that he is to be the next minister. The reckless devil's
disciple of Act I has discovered his positive Christian faith in
the brotherhood of man. Shaw gave him a temperament that
might well rise to the danger of the arrest, the trial, and the
challenge of death itself. It is hardly the temperament to withdraw from action and danger and settle merely to preaching.

Essie has a smaller part than Anderson, Judith, or Mrs Dudgeon. She belongs in the group of puritans as their victim rather
than as one of them. Lying on the sofa by the hearth, in her
ragged and dirty clothes, and scolded by Mrs Dudgeon, she
might well remind us of Cinderella. Having her on stage in
Act I enables Shaw to show a side of Dick Dudgeon that prepares
for his behaviour later in the play; certainly her attitude to
him, and his to her, will influence a reader's or audience's feelings
towards Dick in this Act. The neglected, or ill-treated, orphan
is a pathetic character of a type that the Victorians liked reading
about in their novels and seeing in their melodramas, when
they went to the theatre. Bringing her in at the beginning of
the play strikes a note of sentiment that accords with Shaw's
intention of trying his hand as a writer of melodrama. Essie
does not seem to represent any abstract idea. Evidently, Shaw
does not always use his characters in the same way, or for the
same purposes.

Satire

Shaw did not keep to melodrama throughout *The Devil's Disciple*.

Dick's encounter with the puritans in Act I highlights their faults and general unattractiveness. His mockery of them is satirical, attacking them by making them look ridiculous. This approach is foreign to melodrama, as it disperses sentimentality and even the simple human feeling Shaw himself recognized to be characteristic of the best melodramas. Dick is striking a pose, and those who accept it play into his hands: he has set up the scene and they let him dominate it. This is not the sincerity and straightforwardness of the typical hero of melodrama. Anderson sees what is happening and is not taken in by Dick; his detached presence in the scene ensures that the audience is aware that Dick is showing off and playing a game with the others. Arousing this kind of awareness is part of the method of comedy, which dissolves other emotions in mirth, rather than of melodrama, which seeks to swamp its audience with emotions.

Burgoyne is a character who would be out of place in any other kind of drama than comedy. His elaborate, artificial manner and his formal, witty speeches keep feeling at bay, while he is adept at ridiculing others, as when he remarks (page 74):

It is making too much of the fellow to execute him ... Martyrdom, sir, is what these people like: it is the only way in which a man can become famous without ability

or turns on his junior officer (page 75):

May I ask are you writing a melodrama, Major Swindon?

He dominates much of the last Act, as Richard dominated the first. He, too, is posing and he does it with a polish of manner that outdoes Dick, though the latter plays up to him very well in the trial scene and, indeed, his line, 'I never expect a soldier to think, sir,' could have come from Burgoyne himself. The General's delight at it is as appreciative of its style as of its content. Soldiers and politicians bear the brunt of the satiric mockery

in Act III: not the ordinary soldiers, but the hide-bound pro-
fessionals, whom Major Swindon represents. This is a character
hardly individualized at all, even a puppet-figure to have shots
aimed at him, as if he was in a Punch-and-Judy show. It is a
character drawn with the simple lines of a comic caricature.

The balance of the play

Bernard Shaw is sometimes criticized for creating caricatures
instead of realistic characters that give the illusion of being real
people. The criticism is misguided, unless the general nature
of the play calls only for characters of this type. A play designed
to make us see opposite points of view may present these more
clearly and vividly through characters tailored to express and
demonstrate different attitudes or particular ideas. It is by no
means impossible for unrealistic characters, or caricatures, to
engage our sympathies: reactions to the Pink Panther or Rupert
Bear show that. However, the simple, sincere human emotion
that melodrama at its best is able to communicate does need
some characters that we can readily accept as living, suffering,
rejoicing people, who draw us into their own moods. Most of the
characters in *The Devil's Disciple* are of this kind and, through
them, Shaw is able to strike a balance between the elements of
thought and emotion, between wit and humour, on the one hand,
and the sense of real life, sometimes sad, sometimes grim, on the
other.

It is worth looking back over the play for moments, or whole
scenes, when particular characters are in the grip of feelings
that affect us: for instance, there is the bitterness of Mrs Dudgeon,
her resentment of Anderson's marriage, the force of Dick's
unyielding rejection of his mother, which is his bitter response
to her failure, or refusal, to show him love; the relationship
between Christy and his mother does not have this intensity,
and it may be worth remembering what Anderson says about
the closeness of hate to love. Judith is made tongue-tied and

inarticulate by her confused emotions, torn as she is between fear, affection and loyalty towards her husband and attraction, horror and something like hero-worship of Dick, to which may be added a sense of overwhelming responsibility for what is happening and inability to stop it.

Shaw constructs his plays carefully, but not mechanically, to convey the truths he wants to suggest, but also to keep audiences and readers interested and excited by surprise and variety and, in this play, by keeping the plot moving swiftly, without lapses of tension. We cannot easily separate out what is thoughtful from what is amusing in his work: the two qualities go together; and, though he certainly wants to make *us* think, he usually prevents our thinking from being totally untouched by feeling.

Appendix

The Devil's Disciple *for the screen*

A number of Bernard Shaw's plays have been turned into films, and he himself collaborated in the making of several. The most successful of these were *Pygmalion* (1938) and *Major Barbara* (1941). Plans for filming *The Devil's Disciple* were seriously considered on two occasions during the dramatist's lifetime. On both occasions, the leading American actor of his generation, John Barrymore, wanted to play Dick Dudgeon.

The first plan was for a silent film, using Shaw's dialogue for the captions. Then, in 1934, negotiations with a Hollywood company, RKO, over a talkie version reached the point where a filmscript, prepared by the studio's script writer, Lester Cohen, was submitted to Shaw for his approval. But Shaw was very far from approving, and the RKO film was never made. (A second actor under consideration for the role of Dick Dudgeon in 1934 was Clark Gable, whom Shaw had met and who was noted as available to make the film.)

Eventually, the American Hecht-Hill-Lancaster Company filmed *The Devil's Disciple* in England in 1959, after Shaw's death. The leading actors were Kirk Douglas, Burt Lancaster and Laurence Olivier (as General Burgoyne). The existence of Shaw's own suggestions for the adaptation of his play for the screen was ignored by this company, and the result is generally considered among the least successful films of Shaw plays – except for Olivier's performance.

Shaw believed that preparing a filmscript should be seen by any playwright as part of his proper business, and indeed he was awarded an 'Oscar' for his screenplay of *Pygmalion*. The beginning of a screenplay of his own for *The Devil's Disciple* survived among his papers and has been published in *The Collected Screenplays of Bernard Shaw*, edited by B.F. Dukore (1980). Shaw wanted the film to start by showing the signing of the American Declaration of Independence, and he wrote new dialogue for a scene between King George III and Lord North, in London, to be followed by another that made clear the trivial cause of delay in sending General Howe his instructions. The film was then to cut to shots of Burgoyne's army on the march, before the introduction of Mrs Dudgeon's kitchen and the first lines of the original play text.

The Devil's Disciple

CHARACTERS

in the order of their appearance

MRS DUDGEON

THE GIRL/ESSIE

CHRISTY

ANTHONY ANDERSON

JUDITH ANDERSON

LAWYER HAWKINS

UNCLE WILLIAM DUDGEON

UNCLE TITUS DUDGEON

RICHARD DUDGEON

MRS WILLIAM DUDGEON

MRS TITUS DUDGEON

THE SERGEANT

MAJOR SWINDON

GENERAL BURGOYNE

CHAPLAIN/MR BRUDENELL

SOLDIERS

SHAW'S PREFACE

WHY FOR PURITANS? [1]

SINCE I gave my Plays, Pleasant and Unpleasant, to the world two years ago, many things have happened to me. I had then just entered on the fourth year of my activity as a critic of the London theatres. They very nearly killed me. I had survived seven years of London's music, four or five years of London's pictures, and about as much of its current literature, wrestling critically with them with all my force and skill. After that, the criticism of the theatre came to me as a huge relief in point of bodily exertion. The difference between the leisure of a Persian cat and the labor of a cockney cab horse is not greater than the difference between the official weekly or fortnightly playgoings of the theatre critic and the restless daily rushing to and fro of the music critic, from the stroke of three in the afternoon, when the concerts begin, to the stroke of twelve at night, when the opera ends. The pictures were nearly as bad. An Alpinist once, noticing the massive soles of my boots, asked me whether I climbed mountains. No, I replied: these boots are for the hard floors of the London galleries. Yet I once dealt with music and pictures together in the spare time of an active young revolutionist, and wrote plays and books and other toilsome things into the bargain. But the theatre struck me down like the veriest weakling. I sank under it like a baby fed on starch. My very bones began to perish, so that I had to get them planed and gouged by accomplished surgeons. I fell from heights and broke my limbs in pieces. The doctors said: This man has not eaten meat for twenty years: he must eat it or die. I said: This man has been going to the London theatres for

[1] *The Devil's Disciple*, written in 1897, was published in *Three Plays for Puritans* in 1900, together with *Caesar and Cleopatra* and *Captain Brassbound's Conversion*. The present edition omits the last section of Shaw's Preface, headed 'Better than Shakespear?' and relating only to *Caesar and Cleopatra*.

three years; and the soul of him has become inane and is feeding unnaturally on his body. And I was right. I did not change my diet; but I had myself carried up into a mountain where there was no theatre; and there I began to revive. Too weak to work, I wrote books and plays: hence the second and third plays in this volume. And now I am stronger than I have been at any moment since my feet first carried me as a critic across the fatal threshold of a London playhouse.

Why was this? What is the matter with the theatre, that a strong man can die of it? Well, the answer will make a long story; but it must be told. And, to begin, why have I just called the theatre a playhouse? The well-fed Englishman, though he lives and dies a schoolboy, cannot play. He cannot even play cricket or football: he has to work at them: that is why he beats the foreigner who plays at them. To him playing means playing the fool. He can hunt and shoot and travel and fight: he can, when special holiday festivity is suggested to him, eat and drink, dice and drab, smoke and lounge. But play he cannot. The moment you make his theatre a place of amusement instead of a place of edification, you make it, not a real playhouse, but a place of excitement for the sportsman and the sensualist.

However, this well-fed grown-up-schoolboy Englishman counts for little in the modern metropolitan audience. In the long lines of waiting playgoers lining the pavements outside our fashionable theatres every evening, the men are only the currants in the dumpling. Women are in the majority; and women and men alike belong to that least robust of all our social classes, the class which earns from eighteen to thirty shillings a week in sedentary employment, and lives in lonely lodgings or in drab homes with nagging relatives. These people preserve the innocence of the theatre: they have neither the philosopher's impatience to get to realities (reality being the one thing they want to escape from), nor the longing of the sportsman for violent action, nor the full-fed, experienced, disillusioned sensuality of the rich man, whether he be gentleman or sporting publican.

They read a good deal, and are at home in the fool's paradise of popular romance. They love the pretty man and the pretty woman, and will have both of them fashionably dressed and exquisitely idle, posing against backgrounds of drawing room and dainty garden; in love, but sentimentally, romantically; always ladylike and gentlemanlike. Jejunely insipid, all this, to the stalls, which are paid for (when they *are* paid for) by people who have their own dresses and drawing rooms, and know them to be a mere masquerade behind which there is nothing romantic, and little that is interesting to most of the masqueraders except the clandestine play of natural licentiousness.

The stalls cannot be fully understood without taking into account the absence of the rich evangelical English merchant and his family, and the presence of the rich Jewish merchant and *his* family. I can see no validity whatever in the view that the influence of the rich Jews on the theatre is any worse than the influence of the rich of any other race. Other qualities being equal, men become rich in commerce in proportion to the intensity and exclusiveness of their desire for money. It may be a misfortune that the purchasing power of men who value money above art, philosophy, and the welfare of the whole community, should enable them to influence the theatre (and everything else in the market); but there is no reason to suppose that their influence is any nobler when they imagine themselves Christians than when they know themselves Jews. All that can fairly be said of the Jewish influence on the theatre is that it is exotic, and is not only a customer's influence but a financier's influence: so much so, that the way is smoothest for those plays and those performers that appeal specially to the Jewish taste. English influence on the theatre, as far as the stalls are concerned, does not exist, because the rich purchasing-powerful Englishman prefers politics and church-going: his soul is too stubborn to be purged by an avowed make-believe. When he wants sensuality he practises it: he does not play with voluptuous or romantic ideas. From the play of ideas—and the drama can never be anything more—he demands edification, and will not pay for anything else in that arena. Consequently the box office will never become an English influence until the theatre turns from the drama of romance and sensuality to the drama of edification.

Turning from the stalls to the whole auditorium, consider what is implied by the fact that the prices (all much too high, by the way) range from half a guinea to a shilling, the ages from eighteen to eighty, whilst every age, and nearly every price, represents a different taste. Is it not clear that this diversity in the audience makes it impossible to gratify every one of its units by the same luxury, since in that domain of infinite caprice, one man's meat is another man's poison, one age's longing another age's loathing? And yet that is just what the theatres kept trying to do almost all the time I was doomed to attend them. On the other hand, to interest people of divers ages, classes, and temperaments by some generally momentous subject of thought, as the politicians and preachers do, would seem the most obvious course in the world. And yet the theatres avoided that as a ruinous eccentricity. Their wiseacres persisted in assuming that all men have the same tastes, fancies, and qualities of passion; that no two have the same interests; and that most playgoers have no interests at all. This being precisely contrary to the obvious facts, it followed that the majority of the plays produced were failures, recognizable as such before the end of the first act by the very wiseacres aforementioned, who, quite incapable of understanding the lesson, would thereupon set to work to obtain and produce a play applying their theory still more strictly, with proportionately more disastrous results. The sums of money I saw thus transferred from the pockets of theatrical speculators and syndicates to those of wigmakers, costumiers, scene painters, carpenters, doorkeepers, actors, theatre landlords, and all the other people for whose exclusive benefit most London theatres seem to exist, would have kept a theatre devoted exclusively to the highest drama open all the year round. If the Browning and Shelley Societies were fools, as the wiseacres said they were, for producing Strafford, Colombe's Birthday, and The Cenci; if the Independent Theatre, the New Century Theatre, and the Stage Society are impracticable faddists for producing the plays of Ibsen and Maeterlinck, then what epithet is contemptuous enough for the people who produce the would-be popular plays?

The actor-managers were far more successful, because they produced plays that at least pleased themselves, whereas Commerce, with a false theory of how to please everybody, produced plays that pleased nobody. But their occasional personal successes in voluptuous plays, and, in any case, their careful concealment of failure, confirmed the prevalent error, which was exposed fully only when the plays had to stand or fall openly by their own merits. Even Shakespear was played with his brains cut out. In 1896, when Sir Henry Irving was disabled by an accident at a moment when Miss Ellen Terry was too ill to appear, the theatre had to be closed after a brief attempt to rely on the attraction of a Shakespearean play performed by the stock company. This may have been Shakespear's fault: indeed Sir Henry later on complained that he had lost a princely sum by Shakespear. But Shakespear's reply to this, if he were able to make it, would be that the princely sum was spent, not on his dramatic poetry, but on a gorgeous stage ritualism superimposed on reckless mutilations of his text, the whole being addressed to a public as to which nothing is certain except that its natural bias is towards reverence for Shakespear and dislike and distrust of ritualism. No doubt the Irving ritual appealed to a far more cultivated sensuousness and imaginativeness than the musical farces in which our stage Abbots of Misrule pontificated (with the same financially disastrous result); but in both there was the same intentional brainlessness, founded on the same theory that the public did not want brains, did not want to think, did not want anything but pleasure at the theatre. Unfortunately, this theory happens to be true of a certain section of the public. This section, being courted by the theatres, went to them and drove the other people out. It then discovered, as any expert could have foreseen, that the theatre cannot compete in mere pleasuremongering either with the other arts or with matter-of-fact gallantry. Stage pictures are the worst pictures, stage music the worst music, stage scenery the worst scenery within reach of the Londoner. The leading lady or gentleman may be as tempting to the admirer in the pit as the dishes in a cookshop window are to the penniless tramp on the pavement; but people do not, I presume, go to the theatre to be merely tantalized.

The breakdown on the last point was conclusive. For when the managers tried to put their principle of pleasing everybody into practice, Necessity, ever ironical towards Folly, had driven them to seek a universal pleasure to appeal to. And since many have no ear for music or eye for color, the search for universality inevitably flung the managers back on the instinct of sex as the avenue to all hearts. Of course the appeal was a vapid failure. Speaking for my own sex, I can say that the leading lady was not to everybody's taste: her pretty face often became ugly when she tried to make it expressive; her voice lost its charm (if it ever had any) when she had nothing sincere to say; and the stalls, from racial prejudice, were apt to insist on more Rebecca and less Rowena than the pit cared for. It may seem strange, even monstrous, that a man should feel a constant attachment to the hideous witches in Macbeth, and yet yawn at the prospect of spending another evening in the contemplation of a beauteous young leading lady with voluptuous contours and longlashed eyes, painted and dressed to perfection in the latest fashions. But that is just what happened to me in the theatre.

I did not find that matters were improved by the lady pretending to be "a woman with a past," violently oversexed, or the play being called a problem play, even when the manager, and sometimes, I suspect, the very author, firmly believed the word problem to be the latest euphemism for what Justice Shallow called a bona roba, and certainly would not either of them have staked a farthing on the interest of a genuine problem. In fact these so-called problem plays invariably depended for their dramatic interest on foregone conclusions of the most heartwearying conventionality concerning sexual morality. The authors had no problematic views: all they wanted was to capture some of the fascination of Ibsen. It seemed to them that most of Ibsen's heroines were naughty ladies. And they tried to produce Ibsen plays by making their heroines naughty. But they took great care to make them pretty and expensively dressed. Thus the pseudo-Ibsen play was nothing but the ordinary sensuous ritual of the stage become as frankly pornographic as good manners allowed.

I found that the whole business of stage sensuousness, whether as Lyceum Shakespear, musical farce, or sham Ibsen, finally disgusted me, not because I was Pharisaical, or intolerantly refined, but because I was bored; and boredom is a condition which makes men as susceptible to disgust and irritation as headache makes them to noise and glare. Being a man, I have my share of the masculine silliness and vulgarity on the subject of sex which so astonishes women, to whom sex is a serious matter. I am not an archbishop, and do not pretend to pass my life on one plane or in one mood, and that the highest: on the contrary, I am, I protest, as accessible to the humors of The Rogue's Comedy or The Rake's Progress as to the pious decencies of The Sign of the Cross. Thus Falstaff, coarser than any of the men in our loosest plays, does not bore me: Doll Tearsheet, more abandoned than any of the women, does not shock me. I admit that Romeo and Juliet would be a duller play if it were robbed of the solitary fragment it has preserved for us of the conversation of the husband of Juliet's nurse. No: my disgust was not mere thinskinned prudery. When my moral sense revolted, as it often did to the very fibres, it was invariably at the nauseous compliances of the theatre with conventional virtue. If I despised the musical farces, it was because they never had the courage of their vices. With all their labored efforts to keep up an understanding of furtive naughtiness between the low comedian on the stage and the drunken undergraduate in the stalls, they insisted all the time

7

on their virtue and patriotism and loyalty as pitifully as a poor girl of the pavement will pretend to be a clergyman's daughter. True, I may have been offended when a manager, catering for me with coarse frankness as a slave dealer caters for a Pasha, invited me to forget the common bond of humanity between me and his company by demanding nothing from them but a gloatably voluptuous appearance. But this extreme is never reached at our better theatres. The shop assistants, the typists, the clerks, who, as I have said, preserve the innocence of the theatre, would not dare to let themselves be pleased by it. Even if they did, they would not get it from our reputable managers, who, when faced with the only logical conclusion from their principle of making the theatre a temple of pleasure, indignantly refuse to change the theatrical profession for Mrs Warren's. For that is what all this demand for pleasure at the theatre finally comes to; and the answer to it is, not that people ought not to desire sensuous pleasure (they cannot help it) but that the theatre cannot give it to them, even to the extent permitted by the honor and conscience of the best managers, because a theatre is so far from being a pleasant or even a comfortable place that only by making us forget ourselves can it prevent us from realizing its inconveniences. A play that does not do this for the pleasure-seeker allows him to discover that he has chosen a disagreeable and expensive way of spending the evening. He wants to drink, to smoke, to change the spectacle, to get rid of the middle-aged actor and actress who are boring him, and to see shapely young dancing girls and acrobats doing more amusing things in a more plastic manner. In short, he wants the music hall; and he goes there, leaving the managers astonished at this unexpected but quite inevitable result of the attempt to please him. Whereas, had he been enthralled by the play, even with horror, instead of himself enthralling with the dread of his displeasure the manager, the author and the actors, all had been well. And so we must conclude that the theatre is a place which people can endure only when they forget themselves: that is, when their attention is entirely captured, their interest thoroughly aroused, their sympathies raised to the eagerest readiness, and their selfishness utterly annihilated. Imagine, then, the result of conducting theatres on the principle of appealing exclusively to the instinct of self-gratification in people without power of attention, without interests, without sympathy: in short, without brains or heart. That is how they were conducted whilst I was writing about them; and that is how they nearly killed me.

Yet the managers mean well. Their self-respect is in excess rather than in defect; for they are in full reaction against the Bohemianism of past generations of actors, and so bent on compelling social recognition by a blameless respectability, that the drama, neglected in the struggle, is only just beginning to stir feebly after standing still in England from Tom Robertson's time in the sixties until the first actor was knighted in the nineties. The manager may not want good plays; but he does not want bad plays: he wants nice ones. Nice plays, with nice dresses, nice drawing rooms and nice people, are indispensable: to be ungenteel is worse than to fail. I use the word ungenteel purposely; for the stage presents life on thirty pounds a day, not as it is, but as it is conceived by the earners of thirty shillings a week. The real thing would shock the audience exactly as the manners of the public school and university shock a Board of Guardians. In just the same way, the plays which constitute the genuine aristocracy of modern dramatic literature shock the reverence for gentility which governs our theatres today. For instance, the objection to Ibsen is not really an objection to his philosophy: it is a protest against the fact that his characters do not behave as ladies and gentlemen are popularly supposed to behave. If you adore Hedda Gabler in real life, if you envy her and feel that nothing but your poverty prevents you from being as exquisite a creature, if you know that the accident of matrimony (say with an officer of the guards who falls in love with you across the counter whilst you are reckoning the words in his telegram) may at any moment put you in her place, Ibsen's exposure of the worthlessness and meanness of her life is cruel and blasphemous to you. This point of view is not caught by the clever ladies of Hedda's own class, who recognize the portrait, applaud its painter, and think the fuss against Ibsen means nothing more than the conventional disapproval of her discussions of a *ménage a trois* with Judge Brack. A little experience of popular plays would soon convince these clever ladies that a heroine who atones in the last act by committing suicide may do all the things that Hedda only talked about, without a word of remonstrance from the press or the public. It is not murder, not adultery, not rapine that is objected to: quite the contrary. It is an unladylike attitude towards life: in other words, a disparagement of the social ideals of the poorer middle class and of the vast reinforcements it has had from the working class during the last twenty years. Let but the attitude of the author be gentlemanlike, and his heroines may do what they please. Mrs Tanqueray was received with delight by the public: Saint Teresa would have been hissed off the same stage for her contempt for the ideal represented by a carriage, a fashionable dressmaker, and a dozen servants.

Here, then, is a pretty problem for the manager. He is convinced that plays must depend for their dramatic force on appeals to the sex instinct; and yet he owes it to his own newly conquered social position that they shall be perfectly genteel plays, fit for churchgoers. The sex instinct must therefore proceed upon genteel assumptions. Impossible! you will exclaim. But you are wrong: nothing is more astonishing than the extent to which, in real life, the sex instinct does so proceed, even when the consequence is its lifelong starvation. Few of us have vitality enough to make any of our instincts imperious: we can be made to live on pretences, as the masterful minority well know. But the timid majority, if it rules nowhere else, at least rules in the theatre: fitly enough too, because on the stage pretence is all that can exist. Life has its realities behind its shows: the theatre has nothing but its shows. But can the theatre make a show of lovers' endearments? A thousand times no: perish the thought of such unladylike, ungentlemanlike exhibitions. You can have fights, rescues, conflagrations, trials-at-law, avalanches, murders and executions all directly simulated on the stage if you will. But any such realistic treatment of the incidents of sex is quite out of the question. The singer, the dramatic dancer, the exquisite declaimer of impassioned poesy, the rare artist who, bringing something of the art of all three to the ordinary work of the theatre, can enthral an audience by the expression of dramatic feeling alone, may take love for a theme on the stage; but the prosaic walking gentleman of our fashionable theatres, realistically simulating the incidents of life, cannot touch it without indecorum.

Can any dilemma be more complete? Love is assumed to be the only theme that touches all your audience infallibly, young and old, rich and poor. And yet love is the one subject that the drawing room drama dare not present.

Out of this dilemma, which is a very old one, has come the romantic play: that is, the play in which love is carefully kept off the stage, whilst it is alleged as the motive of all the actions presented to the audience. The result is, to me at least, an intolerable perversion of human conduct. There are two classes of stories that seem to me to be not only fundamentally false but sordidly base. One is the pseudo-religious story, in which the hero or heroine does good on strictly commercial grounds, reluctantly exercising a little virtue on earth in consideration of receiving in return an exorbitant payment in heaven: much as if an odalisque were to allow a cadi to whip her for a couple of millions in gold. The other is the romance in which the hero, also rigidly commercial, will do nothing except for the sake of the heroine. Surely this is as depressing as it is unreal. Compare with it the treatment of love, frankly indecent according to our notions, in oriental fiction. In the Arabian Nights we have a series of stories, some of them very good ones, in which no sort of decorum is observed. The result is that they are infinitely more instructive and enjoyable than our romances, because love is treated in them as naturally as any other passion. There is no cast iron convention as to its effects; no false association of general depravity of character with its corporealities or of general elevation with its sentimentalities; no pretence that a man or woman cannot be courageous and kind and friendly unless infatuatedly in love with somebody (is no poet manly enough to sing The Old Maids of England?): rather, indeed, an insistence on the blinding and narrowing power of lovesickness to make princely heroes unhappy and unfortunate. These tales expose, further, the delusion that the interest of this most capricious, most transient, most easily baffled of all instincts, is inexhaustible, and that the field of the English romancer has been cruelly narrowed by the restrictions under which he is permitted to deal with it. The Arabian storyteller, relieved of all such restrictions, heaps character on character, adventure on adventure, marvel on marvel; whilst the English novelist, like the starving tramp who can think of nothing but his hunger, seems to be unable to escape from the obsession of sex, and will rewrite the very gospels because the originals are not written in the sensuously ecstatic style. At the instance of Martin Luther we long ago gave up imposing celibacy on our priests; but we still impose it on our art, with the very undesirable and unexpected result that no editor, publisher, or manager, will now accept a story or produce a play without "love interest" in it. Take, for a recent example, Mr H. G. Wells's War of the Worlds, a tale of the invasion of the earth by the inhabitants of the planet Mars: a capital story, not to be laid down until finished. Love interest is impossible on its scientific plane: nothing could be more impertinent and irritating. Yet Mr Wells has had to pretend that the hero is in love with a young lady manufactured for the purpose, and to imply that it is on her account alone that he feels concerned about the apparently inevitable destruction of the human race by the Martians. Another example. An American novelist, recently deceased, made a hit some years ago by compiling a Bostonian Utopia from the prospectuses of the little bands of devout Communists who have from time to time, since the days of Fourier and Owen, tried to establish millennial colonies outside our commercial civilization. Even in this economic Utopia we find the inevitable love affair. The hero, waking up in a distant future from a miraculous sleep, meets a Boston young lady, provided expressly for him to fall in love with. Women have by that time given up wearing skirts; but she, to spare his delicacy, gets one out of a museum of antiquities to wear in his presence until he is hardened to the customs of the new age. When I came to that touching incident, I became as Paolo and Francesca: "in that book I read no more." I will not multiply examples: if such unendurable follies occur in the sort of story made by working out a meteorological or economic hypothesis, the extent to which it is carried in sentimental romances needs no expatiation.

The worst of it is that since man's intellectual consciousness of himself is derived from the descriptions of him in books, a persistent misrepresentation of humanity in literature gets finally accepted and acted upon. If every mirror reflected our noses twice their natural size, we should live and die in the faith that we were all Punches; and we should scout a true mirror as the work of a fool, madman, or jester. Nay, I believe we should, by Lamarckian adaptation, enlarge our noses to the admired size; for I have noticed that when a certain type of feature appears in painting and is admired as beautiful, it presently becomes common in nature; so that the Beatrices and Francescas in the picture galleries of one generation, to whom minor poets address verses entitled To My Lady, come to life as the parlormaids and waitresses of the next. If the conventions of romance are only insisted on long enough and uniformly enough (a condition guaranteed by the uniformity of human folly and vanity), then, for the huge compulsorily schooled masses who read romance or nothing, these conventions will become the laws of personal honor. Jealousy, which is either an egotistical meanness or a specific mania, will become obligatory; and ruin, ostracism, breaking up of homes, duelling, murder, suicide and infanticide will be produced (often have been produced, in fact) by incidents which, if left to the operation of natural and right feeling, would produce nothing worse than an hour's soon-forgotten fuss. Men will be slain needlessly on the field of battle because officers conceive it to be their first duty to make romantic exhibitions of conspicuous gallantry. The squire who has never spared an hour from the hunting field to do a little public work on a parish council will be cheered as a patriot because he is willing to kill and get killed for the sake of conferring himself as an institution on other countries. In the courts cases will be argued, not on juridical but on romantic principles; and vindictive damages and vindictive sentences, with the acceptance of nonsensical, and the repudiation or suppression of sensible testimony, will destroy the very sense of law. Kaisers, generals, judges, and prime ministers will set the example of playing to the gallery. Finally the people, now that their compulsory literacy enables every penman to play on their romantic illusions, will be led by the nose far more completely than they ever were by playing on their former ignorance and superstition. Nay, why should I say will be? they *are*. Ten years of cheap reading have changed the English from the most stolid nation in Europe to the most theatrical and hysterical.

It is clear now, why the theatre was insufferable to me; why it left its black mark on my bones as it has left its black mark on the character of the nation; why I call the Puritans to rescue it again as they rescued it before when its foolish pursuit of pleasure sunk it in "profaneness and immorality"? I have, I think, always been a Puritan in my attitude towards Art. I am as fond of fine music and handsome building as Milton was, or Cromwell, or Bunyan; but if I found that they were becoming the instruments of a systematic idolatry of sensuousness, I would hold it good statesmanship to blow every cathedral in the world to pieces with dynamite, organ and all, without the least heed to the screams of the art critics and cultured voluptuaries. And when I see that the nineteenth century has crowned the idolatry of Art with the deification of Love, so that every poet is supposed to have pierced to the holy of holies when he has announced that Love is the Supreme, or the Enough, or the All, I feel that Art was safer in the hands of the most fanatical of Cromwell's major generals than it will be if ever it gets into mine. The pleasures of the senses I can sympathize with and share; but the substitution of sensuous ecstasy for intellectual activity and honesty is the very devil. It has already brought us to Flogging Bills in Parliament, and, by reaction, to androgynous heroes on the stage; and if the infection spreads until the democratic attitude becomes thoroughly Romanticist, the country will become unbearable for all realists, Philistine or Platonic. When it comes to that, the brute force of the strong-minded Bismarckian man of action, impatient of humbug, will combine with the subtlety and spiritual energy of the man of thought whom shams cannot illude or interest. That combination will be on one side; and Romanticism will be on the other. In which event, so much the worse for Romanticism, which will come down even if it has to drag Democracy down with it. For all institutions have in the long run to live by the nature of things, and not by childish pretendings.

ON DIABOLONIAN ETHICS

There is a foolish opinion prevalent that an author should allow his works to speak for themselves, and that he who appends and prefixes explanations to them is likely to be as bad an artist as the painter cited by Cervantes, who wrote under his picture This is a Cock, lest there should be any mistake about it. The pat retort to this thoughtless comparison is that the painter invariably does so label his picture. What is a Royal Academy catalogue but a series of statements that This is The Vale of Rest, This The Shaving of Samson, This Chill October, This H.R.H. The Prince of Wales, and so on? The reason most playwrights do not publish their plays with prefaces is that they cannot write them, the business of intellectually conscious philosopher and skilled critic being no necessary part of their craft. Naturally, making a virtue of their incapacity, they either repudiate prefaces as shameful, or else, with a modest air, request some popular critic to supply one, as much as to say, Were I to tell the truth about myself I must needs seem vainglorious: were I to tell less than the truth I should do myself an injustice and deceive my readers. As to the critic thus called in from the outside, what can he do but imply that his friend's transcendent ability as a dramatist is surpassed only by his beautiful nature as a man? Now what I say is, why should I get another man to praise me when I can praise myself? I have no disabilities to plead: produce me your best critic, and I will criticize his head off. As to philosophy, I taught my critics the little they know in my Quintessence of Ibsenism; and now they turn their guns—the guns I loaded for them—on me, and proclaim that I write as if mankind had intellect without will, or heart, as they call it. Ingrates: who was it that directed your attention to the distinction between Will and Intellect? Not Schopenhauer, I think, but Shaw.

Again, they tell me that So-and-So, who does not write prefaces, is no charlatan. Well, I am. I first caught the ear of the British public on a cart in Hyde Park, to the blaring of brass bands, and this not at all as a reluctant sacrifice of my instinct of privacy to political necessity, but because, like all dramatists and mimes of genuine vocation, I am a natural-born mountebank. I am well aware that the ordinary British citizen requires a profession of shame from all mountebanks by way of homage to the sanctity of the ignoble private life to which he is condemned by his incapacity for public life. Thus Shakespear, after proclaiming that Not marble nor the gilded monuments of Princes should outlive his powerful rhyme, would apologize, in the approved taste, for making himself a motley to the view; and the British citizen has ever since quoted the apology and ignored the fanfare. When an actress writes her memoirs, she impresses on you in every chapter how cruelly it tried her feelings to exhibit her person to the public gaze; but she does not forget to decorate the book with a dozen portraits of herself. I really cannot respond to this demand for mock-modesty. I am ashamed neither of my work nor of the way it is done. I like explaining its merits to the huge majority who dont know good work from bad. It does them good; and it does me good, curing me of nervousness, laziness, and snobbishness. I write prefaces as Dryden did, and treatises as Wagner, because I *can*; and I would give half a dozen of Shakespear's plays for one of the prefaces he ought to have written. I leave the delicacies of retirement to those who are gentlemen first and literary workmen afterwards. The cart and trumpet for me.

This is all very well; but the trumpet is an instrument that grows on one; and sometimes my blasts have been so strident that even those who are most annoyed by them have mistaken the novelty of my shamelessness for novelty in my plays and opinions. Take, for instance [the play printed in the present volume] The Devil's Disciple. It does not contain a single even passably novel incident. Every old patron of the Adelphi pit would, were he not beglamored in a way presently to be explained, recognize the reading of the will, the oppressed orphan finding a protector, the arrest, the heroic sacrifice, the court martial, the scaffold, the reprieve at the last moment, as he recognizes beefsteak pudding on the bill of fare at his restaurant. Yet when the play was produced in 1897 in New York by Mr Richard Mansfield, with a success that proves either that the melodrama was built on very safe old lines, or that the American public is composed exclusively of men of genius, the critics, though one said one thing and another another as to the play's merits, yet all agreed that it was novel—*original*, as they put it—to the verge of audacious eccentricity.

Now this, if it applies to the incidents, plot, construction, and general professional and technical qualities of the play, is nonsense; for the truth is, I am in these matters a very old-fashioned playwright. When a good deal of the same talk, both hostile and friendly, was provoked by my last volume of plays, Mr Robert Buchanan, a dramatist who knows what I know and remembers what I remember of the history of the stage, pointed out that the stage tricks by which I gave the younger generation of playgoers an exquisite sense of quaint unexpectedness, had done duty years ago in Cool as a Cucumber, Used Up, and many forgotten farces and comedies of the Byron-Robertson school, in which the imperturbably impudent comedian, afterwards shelved by the reaction to brainless sentimentality, was a stock figure. It is always so more or less: the novelties of one generation are only the resuscitated fashions of the generation before last.

But the stage tricks of The Devil's Disciple are not, like some of those of Arms and the Man, the forgotten ones of the sixties, but the hackneyed ones of our own time. Why, then, were they not recognized? Partly, no doubt, because of my trumpet and cartwheel declamation. The critics were the victims of the long course of hypnotic suggestion by which G.B.S. the journalist manufactured an unconventional reputation for Bernard Shaw the author. In England as elsewhere the spontaneous recognition of really original work begins with a mere handful of people, and propagates itself so slowly that it has become a commonplace to say that genius, demanding bread, is given a stone after its possessor's death. The remedy for this is sedulous advertisement. Accordingly, I have advertized myself so well that I find myself, whilst still in middle life, almost as legendary a person as the Flying Dutchman. Critics, like other people, see what they look for, not what is actually before them. In my plays they look for my legendary qualities, and find originality and brilliancy in my most hackneyed claptraps. Were I to republish Buckstone's Wreck Ashore as my latest comedy, it would be hailed as a masterpiece of perverse paradox and scintillating satire. Not, of course, by the really able critics—for example, you, my friend, now reading this sentence. The illusion that makes *you* think me so original is far subtler than that. The Devil's Disciple has, in truth, a genuine novelty in it. Only, that novelty is not any invention of my own, but simply the novelty of the advanced thought of my day. As such, it will assuredly lose its gloss with the lapse of time, and leave The Devil's Disciple exposed as the threadbare popular melodrama it technically is.

Let me explain (for, as Mr A. B. Walkley has pointed out in his disquisitions on Frames of Mind, I am nothing if not explanatory). Dick Dudgeon, the devil's disciple, is a Puritan of the Puritans. He is brought up in a household where the Puritan religion has died, and become, in its corruption, an excuse for his mother's master passion of hatred in all its phases of cruelty and envy. This corruption has already been dramatized for us by Charles Dickens in his picture of the Clennam household in Little Dorrit: Mrs Dudgeon being a replica of Mrs Clennam with certain circumstantial variations, and perhaps a touch of the same author's Mrs Gargery in Great Expectations. In such a home the young Puritan finds himself starved of religion, which is the most clamorous need of his nature. With all his mother's indomitable selffulness, but with Pity instead of Hatred as his master passion, he pities the devil; takes his side; and champions him, like a true Covenanter, against the world. He thus becomes, like all genuinely religious men, a reprobate and an outcast. Once this is understood, the play becomes straightforwardly simple.

The Diabolonian position is new to the London playgoer of today, but not to lovers of serious literature. From Prometheus to the Wagnerian Siegfried, some enemy of the gods, unterrified champion of those oppressed by them, has always towered among the heroes of the loftiest poetry. Our newest idol, the Superman, celebrating the death of godhead, may be younger than the hills; but he is as old as the shepherds. Two and a half centuries ago our greatest English dramatizer of life, John Bunyan, ended one of his stories with the remark that there is a way to hell even from the gates of heaven, and so led us to the equally true proposition that there is a way to heaven even from the gates of hell. A century ago William Blake was, like Dick Dudgeon, an avowed Diabolonian: he called his angels devils and his devils angels. His devil is a Redeemer. Let those who have praised my originality in conceiving Dick Dudgeon's strange religion read Blake's Marriage of

Heaven and Hell, and I shall be fortunate if they do not rail at me for a plagiarist. But they need not go back to Blake and Bunyan. Have they not heard the recent fuss about Nietzsche and his Good and Evil Turned Inside Out? Mr Robert Buchanan has actually written a long poem of which the Devil is the merciful hero, which poem was in my hands before a word of The Devil's Disciple was written. There never was a play more certain to be written than The Devil's Disciple at the end of the nineteenth century. The age was visibly pregnant with it.

I grieve to have to add that my old friends and colleagues the London critics for the most part shewed no sort of connoisseurship either in Puritanism or in Diabolonianism when the play was performed for a few weeks at a suburban theatre (Kennington) in October 1899 by Mr Murray Carson. They took Mrs Dudgeon at her own valuation as a religious woman because she was detestably disagreeable. And they took Dick as a blackguard on her authority, because he was neither detestable nor disagreeable. But they presently found themselves in a dilemma. Why should a blackguard save another man's life, and that man no friend of his, at the risk of his own? Clearly, said the critics, because he is redeemed by love. All wicked heroes are, on the stage: that is the romantic metaphysic. Unfortunately for this explanation (which I do not profess to understand) it turned out in the third act that Dick was a Puritan in this respect also: a man impassioned only for saving grace, and not to be led or turned by wife or mother, Church or State, pride of life or lust of the flesh. In the lovely home of the courageous, affectionate, practical minister who marries a pretty wife twenty years younger than himself, and turns soldier in an instant to save the man who has saved him, Dick looks round and understands the charm and the peace and the sanctity, but knows that such material comforts are not for him. When the woman nursed in that atmosphere falls in love with him and concludes (like the critics, who somehow always agree with my sentimental heroines) that he risked his life for her sake, he tells her the obvious truth that he would have done as much for any stranger—that the law of his own nature, and no interest nor lust whatsoever, forbad him to cry out that the hangman's noose should be taken off his neck only to be put on another man's.

But then, said the critics, where is the motive? *Why* did Dick save Anderson? On the stage, it appears, people do things for reasons. Off the stage they dont: that is why your penny-in-the-slot heroes, who only work when you drop a motive into them, are so oppressively automatic and uninteresting. The saving of life at the risk of the saver's own is not a common thing: but modern populations are so vast that even the most uncommon things are recorded once a week or oftener. Not one of my critics but has seen a hundred times in his paper how some policeman or fireman or nursemaid has received a medal, or the compliments of a magistrate, or perhaps a public funeral, for risking his or her life to save another's. Has he ever seen it added that the saved was the husband of the woman the saver loved, or was that woman herself, or was even known to the saver as much as by sight? Never. When we want to read of the deeds that are done for love, whither do we turn? To the murder column; and there we are rarely disappointed.

Need I repeat that the theatre critic's professional routine so discourages any association between real life and the stage, that he soon loses the natural habit of referring to the one to explain the other? The critic who discovered a romantic motive for Dick's sacrifice was no mere literary dreamer, but a clever barrister. He pointed out that Dick Dudgeon clearly did adore Mrs Anderson; that it was for her sake that he offered his life to save her beloved husband; and that his explicit denial of his passion was the splendid mendacity of a gentleman whose respect for a married woman, and duty to her absent husband, sealed his passion-palpitating lips. From the moment that this fatally plausible explanation was launched, my play became my critic's play, not mine. Thenceforth Dick Dudgeon every night confirmed the critic by stealing behind Judith, and mutely attesting his passion by surreptitiously imprinting a heart-broken kiss on a stray lock of her hair whilst he uttered the barren denial. As for me, I was just then wandering about the streets of Constantinople, unaware of all these doings. When I returned all was over. My personal relations with the critic and the actor forbad me to curse them. I had not even the chance of publicly forgiving them. They meant well by me; but if they ever write a play, may I be there to explain![1]

SURREY, 1900.

[1] As I pass these pages through the press (September 1900), the critics of Yorkshire are struggling, as against some unholy fascination, with the apparition of Dick Dudgeon on their stage in the person of Forbes Robertson. "A finished scoundrel" is the description which one of them gives of Dick. This is worth recording as an example of the extent to which the moral sense remains dormant in people who are content with the customary formulas for respectable conduct.

THE DEVIL'S DISCIPLE

ACT I

At the most wretched hour between a black night and a wintry morning in the year 1777, Mrs Dudgeon, of New Hampshire, is sitting up in the kitchen and general dwelling room of her farm house on the outskirts of the town of Websterbridge. She is not a prepossessing woman. No woman looks her best after sitting up all night; and Mrs Dudgeon's face, even at its best, is grimly trenched by the channels into which the barren forms and observances of a dead Puritanism can pen a bitter temper and a fierce pride. She is an elderly matron who has worked hard and got nothing by it except dominion and detestation in her sordid home, and an unquestioned reputation for piety and respectability among her neighbors, to whom drink and debauchery are still so much more tempting than religion and rectitude, that they conceive goodness simply as self-denial. This conception is easily extended to others-denial, and finally generalized as covering anything disagreeable. So Mrs Dudgeon, being exceedingly disagreeable, is held to be exceedingly good. Short of flat felony, she enjoys complete license except for amiable weakness of any sort, and is consequently, without knowing it, the most licentious woman in the parish on the strength of never having broken the seventh commandment or missed a Sunday at the Presbyterian church.

The year 1777 is the one in which the passions roused by the breaking-off of the American colonies from England, more by their own weight than by their own will, boiled up to shooting point, the shooting being idealized to the English mind as suppression of rebellion and maintenance of British dominion, and to the American as defence of liberty, resistance to tyranny, and self-sacrifice on the altar of the Rights of Man. Into the merits of these idealizations it is not here necessary to inquire: suffice it to say, without prejudice, that they have convinced both Americans and English that the most highminded course for them to pursue is to kill as many of one *another as possible, and that military operations to that end are in full swing, morally supported by confident requests from the clergy of both sides for the blessing of God on their arms.*

Under such circumstances many other women besides this disagreeable Mrs Dudgeon find themselves sitting up all night waiting for news. Like her, too, they fall asleep towards morning at the risk of nodding themselves into the kitchen fire. Mrs Dudgeon sleeps with a shawl over her head, and her feet on a broad fender of iron laths, the step of the domestic altar of the fireplace, with its huge hobs and boiler, and its hinged arm above the smoky mantelshelf for roasting. The plain kitchen table is opposite the fire, at her elbow, with a candle on it in a tin sconce. Her chair, like all the others in the room, is uncushioned and unpainted; but as it has a round railed back and a seat conventionally moulded to the sitter's curves, it is comparatively a chair of state. The room has three doors, one on the same side as the fireplace, near the corner, leading to the best bedroom; one, at the opposite end of the opposite wall, leading to the scullery and washhouse; and the housedoor, with its latch, heavy lock, and clumsy wooden bar, in the front wall, between the window in its middle and the corner next the bedroom door. Between the door and the window a rack of pegs suggests to the deductive observer that the men of the house are all away, as there are no coats or hats on them. On the other side of the window the clock hangs on a nail, with its white wooden dial, black iron weights, and brass pendulum. Between the clock and the corner, a big cupboard, locked, stands on a dwarf dresser full of common crockery.

On the side opposite the fireplace, between the door and the corner, a shamelessly ugly black horsehair sofa stands against the wall. An inspection of its stridulous surface shews that Mrs Dudgeon is not alone. A girl of sixteen or seventeen has fallen asleep on it. She is a wild, timid looking creature with black hair and tanned skin. Her frock, a scanty garment, is rent, weather-stained, berrystained, and by no means scrupulously clean. It hangs on her with a freedom which, taken with her brown legs and bare feet, suggests no great stock of underclothing.

Suddenly there comes a tapping at the door, not loud enough to wake the sleepers. Then knocking, which disturbs Mrs Dudgeon a little. Finally the latch is tried, whereupon she springs up at once.

MRS DUDGEON [*threateningly*] Well, why dont you open the door? [*She sees that the girl is asleep, and immediately raises a clamor of heartfelt vexation*]. Well, dear, dear me! Now this is— [*shaking her*] wake up, wake up: do you hear?

THE GIRL [*sitting up*] What is it?

MRS DUDGEON. Wake up; and be ashamed of yourself, you unfeeling sinful girl, falling asleep like that, and your father hardly cold in his grave.

THE GIRL [*half asleep still*] I didnt mean to. I dropped off—

MRS DUDGEON [*cutting her short*] Oh yes, youve plenty of excuses, I daresay. Dropped off! [*Fiercely, as the knocking recommences*] Why dont you get up and let your uncle in? after me waiting up all night for him! [*She pushes her rudely off the sofa*]. There: I'll open the door: much good you are to wait up. Go and mend that fire a bit.

The girl, cowed and wretched, goes to the fire and puts a log on. Mrs Dudgeon unbars the door and opens it, letting into the stuffy kitchen a little of the freshness and a great deal of the chill of the dawn, also her second son Christy, a fattish, stupid, fair-haired, roundfaced man of about 22, muffled in a plaid shawl and grey overcoat. He hurries, shivering, to the fire, leaving Mrs Dudgeon to shut the door.

CHRISTY [*at the fire*] F—f—f! but it is cold. [*Seeing the girl, and staring lumpishly at her*] Why, who are you?

THE GIRL [*shyly*] Essie.

MRS DUDGEON. Oh, you may well ask. [*To Essie*] Go to your room, child, and lie down, since you havnt feeling enough to keep you awake. Your history isnt fit for your own ears to hear.

ESSIE. I—

MRS DUDGEON [*peremptorily*] Dont answer me, Miss; but shew your obedience by doing what I tell you. [*Essie, almost in tears, crosses the room to the door near the sofa*]. And dont forget your prayers. [*Essie goes out*]. She'd have gone to bed last night just as if nothing had happened if I'd let her.

CHRISTY [*phlegmatically*] Well, she cant be expected to feel Uncle Peter's death like one of the family.

MRS DUDGEON. What are you talking about, child? Isnt she his daughter—the punishment of his wickedness and shame? [*She assaults her chair by sitting down*].

CHRISTY [*staring*] Uncle Peter's daughter!

MRS DUDGEON. Why else should she be here? D'ye think Ive not had enough trouble and care put upon me bringing up my own girls, let alone you and your good-for-nothing brother, without having your uncle's bastards—

CHRISTY [*interrupting her with an apprehensive glance at the door by which Essie went out*] Sh! She may hear you.

MRS DUDGEON [*raising her voice*] Let her hear me. People who fear God dont fear to give the devil's work its right name. [*Christy, soullessly indifferent to the strife of Good and Evil, stares at the fire, warming himself*]. Well, how long are you going to stare there like a stuck pig? What news have you for me?

CHRISTY [*taking off his hat and shawl and going to the rack to hang them up.*] The minister is to break the news to you. He'll be here presently.

MRS DUDGEON. Break what news?

CHRISTY [*standing on tiptoe, from boyish habit, to hang his hat up, though he is quite tall enough to reach the peg, and speaking with callous placidity, considering the nature of the announcement*] Father's dead too.

MRS DUDGEON [*stupent*] Your father!

CHRISTY [*sulkily, coming back to the fire and warming himself again, attending much more to the fire than to his mother*] Well, it's not my fault. When we got to Nevinstown we found him ill in bed. He didnt know us at first. The minister sat up with him and sent me away. He died in the night.

MRS DUGDEON [*bursting into dry angry tears*] Well, I do think

26

this is hard on me—very hard on me. His brother, that was a disgrace to us all his life, gets hanged on the public gallows as a rebel; and your father, instead of staying at home where his duty was, with his own family, goes after him and dies, leaving everything on my shoulders. After sending this girl to me to take care of, too! [*She plucks her shawl vexedly over her ears*]. It's sinful, so it is: downright sinful.

CHRISTY [*with a slow, bovine cheerfulness, after a pause*] I think it's going to be a fine morning, after all.

MRS DUDGEON [*railing at him*] A fine morning! And your father newly dead! Wheres your feelings, child?

CHRISTY [*obstinately*] Well, I didn't mean any harm. I suppose a man may make a remark about the weather even if his father's dead.

MRS DUDGEON [*bitterly*] A nice comfort my children are to me! One son a fool, and the other a lost sinner thats left his home to live with smugglers and gypsies and villains, the scum of the earth!

Someone knocks.

CHRISTY [*without moving*] Thats the minister.

MRS DUDGEON [*sharply*] Well, arnt you going to let Mr Anderson in?

Christy goes sheepishly to the door. Mrs Dudgeon buries her face in her hands, as it is her duty as a widow to be overcome with grief. Christy opens the door, and admits the minister, Anthony Anderson, a shrewd, genial, ready Presbyterian divine of about 50, with something of the authority of his profession in his bearing. But it is an altogether secular authority, sweetened by a conciliatory, sensible manner not at all suggestive of a quite thorough-going other-worldliness. He is a strong, healthy man too, with a thick sanguine neck; and his keen, cheerful mouth cuts into somewhat fleshy corners. No doubt an excellent parson, but still a man capable of making the most of this world, and perhaps a little apologetically conscious of getting on better with it than a sound Presbyterian ought.

ANDERSON [*to Christy, at the door, looking at Mrs Dudgeon whilst he takes off his cloak*] Have you told her?

CHRISTY. She made me. [*He shuts the door; yawns; and loafs across to the sofa, where he sits down and presently drops off to sleep*].

Anderson looks compassionately at Mrs Dudgeon. Then he hangs his cloak and hat on the rack. Mrs Dudgeon dries her eyes and looks up at him.

ANDERSON. Sister: the Lord has laid his hand very heavily upon you.

MRS DUDGEON [*with intensely recalcitrant resignation*] It's His will, I suppose; and I must bow to it. But I do think it hard. What call had Timothy to go to Springtown, and remind everybody that he belonged to a man that was being hanged?—and [*spitefully*] that deserved it, if ever a man did.

ANDERSON [*gently*] They were brothers, Mrs Dudgeon.

MRS DUDGEON. Timothy never acknowledged him as his brother after we were married: he had too much respect for me to insult me with such a brother. Would such a selfish wretch as Peter have come thirty miles to see Timothy hanged, do you think? Not thirty yards, not he. However, I must bear my cross as best I may: least said is soonest mended.

ANDERSON [*very grave, coming down to the fire to stand with his back to it*] Your eldest son was present at the execution, Mrs Dudgeon.

MRS DUDGEON [*disagreeably surprised*] Richard?

ANDERSON [*nodding*] Yes.

MRS DUDGEON [*vindictively*] Let it be a warning to him. He may end that way himself, the wicked, dissolute, godless—[*she suddenly stops; her voice fails; and she asks, with evident dread*] Did Timothy see him?

ANDERSON. Yes.

MRS DUDGEON [*holding her breath*] Well?

ANDERSON. He only saw him in the crowd: they did not speak. [*Mrs Dudgeon, greatly relieved, exhales the pent up breath and sits at her ease again*]. Your husband was greatly touched and impressed by his brother's awful death. [*Mrs Dudgeon sneers. Anderson breaks off to demand with some indignation*] Well, wasnt it only natural, Mrs Dudgeon? He softened towards his prodigal son in that moment. He sent for him to come to see him.

MRS DUDGEON [*her alarm renewed*] Sent for Richard!

ANDERSON. Yes; but Richard would not come. He sent his father a message; but I'm sorry to say it was a wicked message—an awful message.

MRS DUDGEON. What was it?

ANDERSON. That he would stand by his wicked uncle and stand against his good parents, in this world and the next.

MRS DUDGEON [*implacably*] He will be punished for it. He will be punished for it—in both worlds.

ANDERSON. That is not in our hands, Mrs Dudgeon.

MRS DUDGEON. Did I say it was, Mr Anderson? We are told that the wicked shall be punished. Why should we do our duty and keep God's law if there is to be no difference made between us and those who follow their own likings and dislikings, and make a jest of us and of their Maker's word?

ANDERSON. Well, Richard's earthly father has been merciful to him; and his heavenly judge is the father of us all.

MRS DUDGEON [*forgetting herself*] Richard's earthly father was a softheaded—

ANDERSON [*shocked*] Oh!

MRS DUDGEON [*with a touch of shame*] Well, I am Richard's mother. If I am against him who has any right to be for him? [*Trying to conciliate him*] Wont you sit down, Mr Anderson? I should have asked you before; but I'm so troubled.

ANDERSON. Thank you. [*He takes a chair from beside the fireplace, and turns it so that he can sit comfortably at the fire. When he is seated he adds, in the tone of a man who knows that he is opening a difficult subject*] Has Christy told you about the new will?

MRS DUDGEON [*all her fears returning*] The new will! Did Timothy—? [*She breaks off, gasping, unable to complete the question*].

ANDERSON. Yes. In his last hours he changed his mind.

MRS DUDGEON [*white with intense rage*] And you let him rob me?

ANDERSON. I had no power to prevent him giving what was his to his own son.

MRS DUDGEON. He had nothing of his own. His money was the money I brought him as my marriage portion. It was for me to deal with my own money and my own son. He dare not have done it if I had been with him; and well he knew it. That was why he stole away like a thief to take advantage of the law to rob me by making a new will behind my back. The more shame on you, Mr Anderson,—you, a minister of the gospel—to act as his accomplice in such a crime.

ANDERSON [*rising*] I will take no offence at what you say in the first bitterness of your grief.

MRS DUDGEON [*contemptuously*] Grief!

ANDERSON. Well, of your disappointment, if you can find it in your heart to think that the better word.

MRS DUDGEON. My heart! My heart! And since when, pray, have you begun to hold up our hearts as trustworthy guides for us?

ANDERSON [*rather guiltily*] I—er—

MRS DUDGEON [*vehemently*] Dont lie, Mr Anderson. We are told that the heart of man is deceitful above all things, and desperately wicked. My heart belonged, not to Timothy, but to that poor wretched brother of his that has just ended his days with a rope round his neck—aye, to Peter Dudgeon. You know it: old Eli Hawkins, the man to whose pulpit you succeeded, though you are not worthy to loose his shoe latchet, told it you when he gave over our souls into your charge. He warned me and strengthened me against my heart, and made me marry a Godfearing man—as he thought. What else but that discipline has made me the woman I am? And you, you, who followed your heart in your marriage, you talk to me of what I find in my heart. Go home to your pretty wife, man; and leave me to my prayers. [*She turns from him and leans with her elbows on the table, brooding over her wrongs and taking no further notice of him*].

ANDERSON [*willing enough to escape*] The Lord forbid that I should come between you and the source of all comfort! [*He goes to the rack for his coat and hat*].

MRS DUDGEON [*without looking at him*] The Lord will know what to forbid and what to allow without your help.

ANDERSON. And whom to forgive, I hope—Eli Hawkins and myself, if we have ever set up our preaching against His law. [*He fastens his cloak, and is now ready to go.*] Just one word—on necessary business, Mrs Dudgeon. There is the reading of the will to be gone through; and Richard has a right to be present. He is in the town; but he has the grace to say that he does not want to force himself in here.

MRS DUDGEON. He s h a l l come here. Does he expect us to leave his father's house for his convenience? Let them all come, and come quickly, and go quickly. They shall not make the will an excuse to shirk half their day's work. I shall be ready, never fear.

ANDERSON [*coming back a step or two*] Mrs Dudgeon: I used to have some little influence with you. When did I lose it?

MRS DUDGEON [*still without turning to him*] When you married for love. Now youre answered.

ANDERSON. Yes: I am answered. [*He goes out, musing*].

MRS DUDGEON [*to herself, thinking of her husband*] Thief! Thief!! [*She shakes herself angrily out of her chair; throws back the shawl from her head; and sets to work to prepare the room for the reading of the will, beginning by replacing Anderson's chair against the wall, and pushing back her own to the window. Then she calls, in her hard, driving, wrathful way*] Christy. [*No answer: he is fast asleep*]. Christy. [*She shakes him roughly*]. Get up out of that; and be ashamed of yourself—sleeping, and your father dead! [*She returns to the table; puts the candle on the mantelshelf; and takes from the table drawer a red table cloth which she spreads*].

CHRISTY [*rising reluctantly*] Well, do you suppose we are never going to sleep until we are out of mourning?

MRS DUDGEON. I want none of your sulks. Here: help me to set this table. [*They place the table in the middle of the room, with Christy's end towards the fireplace and Mrs Dudgeon's towards the sofa. Christy drops the table as soon as possible, and goes to the fire, leaving his mother to make the final adjustments of its position*]. We shall have the minister back here with the lawyer and all the family to read the will before you have done toasting yourself. Go and wake that girl; and then light the stove in the shed: you cant have your breakfast here. And mind you wash yourself, and make yourself fit to receive the company. [*She punctuates these orders by going to the cupboard; unlocking it; and producing a decanter of wine, which has no doubt stood there untouched since the last state occasion in the family, and some glasses, which she sets on the table. Also two green ware plates, on one of which she puts a barnbrack with a knife beside it. On the other she shakes some biscuits out of a tin, putting back one or two, and counting the rest*]. Now mind: there are ten biscuits there: let there be ten there when I come back after dressing myself. And keep your fingers off the raisins in that cake. And tell Essie the same. I suppose I can trust you to bring in the case of stuffed birds without breaking the glass? [*She replaces the tin in the cupboard, which she locks, pocketing the key carefully*].

CHRISTY [*lingering at the fire*] Youd better put the inkstand instead, for the lawyer.

MRS DUDGEON. Thats no answer to make to me, sir. Go and do as youre told. [*Christy turns sullenly to obey*]. Stop: take down that shutter before you go, and let the daylight in: you cant expect me to do all the heavy work of the house with a great lout like you idling about.

Christy takes the window bar out of its clamps, and puts it aside; then opens the shutter, shewing the grey morning. Mrs Dudgeon takes the sconce from the mantelshelf; blows out the candle; extinguishes the snuff by pinching it with her fingers, first licking them for the purpose; and replaces the sconce on the shelf.

CHRISTY [*looking through the window*] Heres the minister's wife.

MRS DUDGEON [*displeased*] What! Is she coming here?

CHRISTY. Yes.

MRS DUDGEON. What does she want troubling me at this hour, before I am properly dressed to receive people?

CHRISTY. Youd better ask her.

MRS DUDGEON [*threateningly*] Youd better keep a civil tongue in your head. [*He goes sulkily towards the door. She comes after him, plying him with instructions*]. Tell that girl to come to me as soon as she's had her breakfast. And tell her to make herself fit to be seen before the people. [*Christy goes out and slams the door in her face*]. Nice manners, that! [*Someone knocks at the house door: she turns and cries inhospitably*] Come in. [*Judith Anderson, the minister's wife, comes in. Judith is more than twenty years younger than her husband, though she will never be as young as he in vitality. She is pretty and proper and ladylike, and has been admired and petted into an opinion of herself sufficiently favorable to give her a self-assurance which serves her instead of strength. She has a pretty taste in dress, and in her face the pretty lines of a sentimental character formed by dreams. Even her little self-complacency is pretty, like a child's vanity. Rather a pathetic creature to any sympathetic observer who knows how rough a place the world is. One feels, on the whole, that Anderson might have chosen worse, and that she, needing protection, could not have chosen better*]. Oh, it's you, is it, Mrs Anderson?

JUDITH [*very politely—almost patronizingly*] Yes. Can I do anything for you, Mrs Dudgeon? Can I help to get the place ready before they come to read the will?

MRS DUDGEON [*stiffly*] Thank you, Mrs Anderson, my house is always ready for anyone to come into.

MRS ANDERSON [*with complacent amiability*] Yes, indeed it is. Perhaps you had rather I did not intrude on you just now.

MRS DUDGEON. Oh, one more or less will make no difference this morning, Mrs Anderson. Now that youre here, youd better stay. If you wouldnt mind shutting the door! [*Judith smiles, implying "How stupid of me?" and shuts it with an exasperating air of doing something pretty and becoming*]. Thats better. I must go and tidy myself a bit. I suppose you dont mind stopping here to receive anyone that comes until I'm ready.

JUDITH [*graciously giving her leave*] Oh yes, certainly. Leave that to me, Mrs Dudgeon; and take your time. [*She hangs her cloak and bonnet on the rack*].

MRS DUDGEON [*half sneering*] I thought that would be more in your way than getting the house ready. [*Essie comes back*]. Oh, here you are! [*Severely*] Come here: let me see you. [*Essie timidly goes to her. Mrs Dudgeon takes her roughly by the arm and pulls her round to inspect the results of her attempt to clean and tidy herself—results which shew little practice and less conviction*]. Mm! Thats what you call doing you hair properly, I suppose. It's easy to see what you are, and how you were brought up. [*She throws her arm away, and goes on, peremptorily*] Now you listen to me and do as youre told. You sit down there in the corner by the fire; and when the company comes dont dare to speak until youre spoken to. [*Essie creeps away to the fireplace*]. Your father's people had better see you and know youre there: theyre as much bound to keep you from starvation as I am. At any rate they might help. But let me have no chattering and making free with them, as if you were their equal. Do you hear?

ESSIE. Yes.

MRS DUDGEON. Well, then go and do as youre told. [*Essie sits down miserably on the corner of the fender farthest from the door*]. Never mind her, Mrs Anderson: you know who she is and what she is. If she gives you any trouble, just tell me; and I'll settle accounts with her. [*Mrs Dudgeon goes into the bedroom, shutting the door sharply behind her as if even it had to be made do its duty with a ruthless hand*].

JUDITH [*patronizing Essie, and arranging the cake and wine on the table more becomingly*] You must not mind if your aunt is strict with you. She is a very good woman, and desires your good too.

ESSIE [*in listless misery*] Yes.

JUDITH [*annoyed with Essie for her failure to be consoled and edified, and to appreciate the kindly condescension of the remark*] You are not going to be sullen, I hope, Essie.

ESSIE. No.

JUDITH. Thats a good girl! [*She places a couple of chairs at the table with their backs to the window, with a pleasant sense of being a more thoughtful housekeeper than Mrs Dudgeon*]. Do you know any of your father's relatives?

ESSIE. No. They wouldnt have anything to do with him: they were too religious. Father used to talk about Dick Dudgeon; but I never saw him.

JUDITH [*ostentatiously shocked*] Dick Dudgeon! Essie: do you wish to be a really respectable and grateful girl, and to make a place for yourself here by steady good conduct?

ESSIE [*very half-heartedly*] Yes.

JUDITH. Then you must never mention the name of Richard Dudgeon—never think even about him. He is a bad man.

ESSIE. What has he done?

JUDITH. You must not ask questions about him, Essie. You are too young to know what it is to be a bad man. But he is a smuggler; and he lives with gypsies; and he has no love for his mother and his family; and he wrestles and plays games on Sunday instead of going to church. Never let him into your presence, if you can help it, Essie; and try to keep yourself and all womanhood unspotted by contact with such men.

ESSIE. Yes.

JUDITH [*again displeased*] I am afraid you say Yes and No without thinking very deeply.

ESSIE. Yes. At least I mean—

JUDITH [*severely*] What do you mean?

ESSIE [*almost crying*] Only—my father was a smuggler; and— [*Someone knocks*].

JUDITH. They are beginning to come. Now remember your aunt's directions, Essie; and be a good girl. [*Christy comes back with the stand of stuffed birds under a glass case, and an inkstand, which he places on the table*]. Good morning, Mr Dudgeon. Will you open the door, please: the people have come.

CHRISTY. Good morning. [*He opens the house door*].

The morning is now fairly bright and warm; and Anderson, who is the first to enter, has left his cloak at home. He is accompanied by

THE DEVIL'S DISCIPLE

Lawyer Hawkins, a brisk, middleaged man in brown riding gaiters and yellow breeches, looking as much squire as solicitor. He and Anderson are allowed precedence as representing the learned professions. After them comes the family, headed by the senior uncle, William Dudgeon, a large, shapeless man, bottle-nosed and evidently no ascetic at table. His clothes are not the clothes, nor his anxious wife the wife, of a prosperous man. The junior uncle, Titus Dudgeon, is a wiry little terrier of a man, with an immense and visibly purseproud wife, both free from the cares of the William household.

Hawkins at once goes briskly to the table and takes the chair nearest the sofa, Christy having left the inkstand there. He puts his hat on the floor beside him, and produces the will. Uncle William comes to the fire and stands on the hearth warming his coat tails, leaving Mrs William derelict near the door. Uncle Titus, who is the lady's man of the family, rescues her by giving her his disengaged arm and bringing her to the sofa, where he sits down warmly between his own lady and his brother's. Anderson hangs up his hat and waits for a word with Judith.

JUDITH. She will be here in a moment. Ask them to wait. [*She taps at the bedroom door. Receiving an answer from within, she opens it and passes through*].

ANDERSON [*taking his place at the table at the opposite end to Hawkins*] .Our poor afflicted sister will be with us in a moment. Are we all here?

CHRISTY [*at the house door, which he has just shut*] All except Dick.

The callousness with which Christy names the reprobate jars on the moral sense of the family. Uncle William shakes his head slowly and repeatedly. Mrs Titus catches her breath convulsively through her nose. Her husband speaks.

UNCLE TITUS. Well, I hope he will have the grace not to come. I hope so.

The Dudgeons all murmur assent, except Christy, who goes to the window and posts himself there, looking out. Hawkins smiles secretively as if he knew something that would change their tune if they knew it. Anderson is uneasy: the love of solemn family councils, especially funeral ones, is not in his nature. Judith appears at the bedroom door.

JUDITH [*with gentle impressiveness*] Friends, Mrs Dudgeon. [*She takes the chair from beside the fireplace; and places it for Mrs Dudgeon, who comes from the bedroom in black, with a clean handkerchief to her eyes. All rise, except Essie. Mrs Titus and Mrs William produce equally clean handkerchiefs and weep. It is an affecting moment*].

UNCLE WILLIAM. Would it comfort you, sister, if we were to offer up a prayer?

UNCLE TITUS. Or sing a hymn?

ANDERSON [*rather hastily*] I have been with our sister this morning already, friends. In our hearts we ask a blessing.

ALL [*except Essie*] Amen.

They all sit down, except Judith, who stands behind Mrs Dudgeon's chair.

JUDITH [*to Essie*] Essie: did you say Amen?

ESSIE [*scaredly*] No.

JUDITH. Then say it, like a good girl.

ESSIE. Amen.

UNCLE WILLIAM [*encouragingly*] Thats right: thats right. We know who you are; but we are willing to be kind to you if you are a good girl and deserve it. We are all equal before the Throne.

This republican sentiment does not please the women, who are convinced that the Throne is precisely the place where their superiority, often questioned in this world, will be recognized and rewarded.

CHRISTY [*at the window*] Heres Dick.

Anderson and Hawkins look round sociably. Essie, with a gleam of interest breaking through her misery, looks up. Christy grins and gapes expectantly at the door. The rest are petrified with the intensity of their sense of Virtue menaced with outrage by the approach of flaunting Vice. The reprobate appears in the doorway, graced beyond his alleged merits by the morning sunlight. He is certainly the best looking member of the family; but his expression is reckless and sardonic, his manner defiant and satirical, his dress picturesquely care-less. Only, his forehead and mouth betray an extraordinary steadfast-ness; and his eyes are the eyes of a fanatic.

RICHARD [*on the threshold, taking off his hat*] Ladies and gentle-men: your servant, your very humble servant. [*With this compre-hensive insult, he throws his hat to Christy with a suddenness that makes him jump like a negligent wicket keeper, and comes into the middle of the room, where he turns and deliberately surveys the com-pany*]. How happy you all look! how glad to see me! [*He turns towards Mrs Dudgeon's chair; and his lip rolls up horribly from his dog tooth as he meets her look of undisguised hatred*]. Well, mother: keeping up appearances as usual? thats right, thats right. [*Judith pointedly moves away from his neighborhood to the other side of the kitchen, holding her skirt instinctively as if to save it from contamina-tion. Uncle Titus promptly marks his approval of her action by rising from the sofa, and placing a chair for her to sit down upon*]. What! Uncle William! I havnt seen you since you gave up drinking. [*Poor Uncle William, shamed, would protest; but Richard claps him heartily on his shoulder, adding*] you have given it up, havnt you? [*releasing him with a playful push*] of course you have: quite right too: you overdid it. [*He turns away from Uncle William and makes for the sofa*]. And now, where is that upright horsedealer Uncle Titus? Uncle Titus: come forth. [*He comes upon him holding the chair as Judith sits down*]. As usual, looking after the ladies!

UNCLE TITUS [*indignantly*] Be ashamed of yourself, sir—

RICHARD [*interrupting him and shaking his hand in spite of him*] I am: I am; but I am proud of my uncle—proud of all my relatives —[*again surveying them*] who could look at them and not be proud and joyful? [*Uncle Titus, overborne, resumes his seat on the sofa. Richard turns to the table*]. Ah, Mr Anderson, still at the good work, still shepherding them. Keep them up to the mark, minister, keep them up to the mark. Come! [*with a spring he seats himself on the table and takes up the decanter*] clink a glass with me, Pastor, for the sake of old times.

ANDERSON. You know, I think, Mr Dudgeon, that I do not drink before dinner.

RICHARD. You will, some day, Pastor: Uncle William used to drink before breakfast. Come: it will give your sermons unction. [*He smells the wine and makes a wry face*]. But do not begin on my mother's company sherry. I stole some when I was six years old; and I have been a temperate man ever since. [*He puts the decanter down and changes the subject*]. So I hear you are married, Pastor, and that your wife has a most ungodly allowance of good looks.

ANDERSON [*quietly indicating Judith*] Sir: you are in the presence of my wife. [*Judith rises and stands with stony propriety*].

RICHARD [*quickly slipping down from the table with instinctive good manners*] Your servant, madam: no offence. [*He looks at her earnestly*]. You deserve your reputation; but I'm sorry to see by your expression that youre a good woman. [*She looks shocked, and sits down amid a murmur of indignant sympathy from his relatives. Anderson, sensible enough to know that these demonstrations can only gratify and encourage a man who is deliberately trying to provoke them, remains perfectly goodhumored*]. All the same, Pastor, I respect you more than I did before. By the way, did I hear, or did I not, that our late lamented Uncle Peter, though unmarried, was a father?

UNCLE TITUS. He had only one irregular child, sir.

RICHARD. Only one! He thinks one a mere trifle! I blush for you, Uncle Titus.

ANDERSON. Mr Dudgeon: you are in the presence of your mother and her grief.

RICHARD. It touches me profoundly, Pastor. By the way, what has become of the irregular child?

ANDERSON [*pointing to Essie*] There, sir, listening to you.

RICHARD [*shocked into sincerity*] What! Why the devil didnt you tell me that before? Children suffer enough in this house without—[*He hurries remorsefully to Essie*]. Come, little cousin! never mind me: it was not meant to hurt you. [*She looks up gratefully at him. Her tearstained face affects him violently; and he bursts out, in a transport of wrath*] Who has been making her cry? Who has been ill-treating her? By God—

MRS DUDGEON [*rising and confronting him*] Silence your blasphemous tongue. I will bear no more of this. Leave my house.

RICHARD. How do you know it's your house until the will is read? [*They look at one another for a moment with intense hatred; and then she sinks, checkmated, into her chair. Richard goes boldly up past Anderson to the window, where he takes the railed chair in his hand*]. Ladies and gentlemen: as the eldest son of my late father, and the unworthy head of this household, I bid you welcome. By your leave, Minister Anderson: by your leave, Lawyer Hawkins. The head of the table for the head of the family. [*He places the chair at the table between the minister and the attorney; sits down between them; and addresses the assembly with a presidential air*]. We meet on a melancholy occasion: a father dead! an uncle actually hanged, and probably damned. [*He shakes his head deploringly. The relatives freeze with horror*]. Thats right: pull your longest faces [*his voice suddenly sweetens gravely as his glance lights on Essie*] provided only there is hope in the eyes of the child. [*Briskly*] Now then, Lawyer Hawkins; business, business. Get on with the will, man.

TITUS. Do not let yourself be ordered or hurried, Mr Hawkins.

HAWKINS [*very politely and willingly*] Mr Dudgeon means no offence, I feel sure. I will not keep you one second, Mr Dudgeon. Just while I get my glasses—[*he fumbles for them. The Dudgeons look at one another with misgiving*].

RICHARD. Aha! They notice your civility, Mr Hawkins. They are prepared for the worst. A glass of wine to clear your voice before you begin. [*He pours out one for him and hands it; then pours one for himself*].

HAWKINS. Thank you, Mr Dudgeon, Your good health, sir.

RICHARD. Yours, sir. [*With the glass half way to his lips, he checks himself, giving a dubious glance at the wine, and adds, with quaint intensity*] Will anyone oblige me with a glass of water?

Essie, who has been hanging on his every word and movement,

*rises stealthily and slips out behind Mrs Dudgeon through the bed-
room door, returning presently with a jug and going out of the house
as quietly as possible.*

HAWKINS. The will is not exactly in proper legal phraseology.

RICHARD. No: my father died without the consolations of the law.

HAWKINS. Good again, Mr Dudgeon, good again. [*Preparing to
read*] Are you ready, sir?

RICHARD. Ready, aye ready. For what we are about to receive,
may the Lord make us truly thankful. Go ahead.

HAWKINS [*reading*] "This is the last will and testament of me
Timothy Dudgeon on my deathbed at Nevinstown on the road
from Springtown to Websterbridge on this twenty-fourth day of
September, one thousand seven hundred and seventy seven. I
hereby revoke all former wills made by me and declare that I am
of sound mind and know well what I am doing and that this is my
real will according to my own wish and affections."

RICHARD [*glancing at his mother*] Aha!

HAWKINS [*shaking his head*] Bad phraseology, sir, wrong
phraseology. "I give and bequeath a hundred pounds to my
younger son Christopher Dudgeon, fifty pounds to be paid to him
on the day of his marriage to Sarah Wilkins if she will have him,
and ten pounds on the birth of each of his children up to the
number of five."

RICHARD. How if she wont have him?

CHRISTY. She will if I have fifty pounds.

RICHARD. Good, my brother. Proceed.

HAWKINS. "I give and bequeath to my wife Annie Dudgeon,
born Annie Primrose"—you see he did not know the law, Mr
Dudgeon: your mother was not born Annie: she was christened
so—"an annuity of fifty-two pounds a year for life [*Mrs Dudgeon,
with all eyes on her, holds herself convulsively rigid*] to be paid out
of the interest on her own money"—theres a way to put it, Mr
Dudgeon! Her own money!

MRS DUDGEON. A very good way to put God's truth. It was
every penny my own. Fifty-two pounds a year!

41

HAWKINS. "And I recommend her for her goodness and piety to the forgiving care of her children, having stood between them and her as far as I could to the best of my ability."

MRS DUDGEON. And this is my reward! [*Raging inwardly*] You know what I think, Mr Anderson: you know the word I gave to it.

ANDERSON. It cannot be helped, Mrs Dudgeon. We must take what comes to us. [*To Hawkins*]. Go on, sir.

HAWKINS. "I give and bequeath my house at Websterbridge with the land belonging to it and all the rest of my property so-ever to my eldest son and heir, Richard Dudgeon."

RICHARD. Oho! The fatted calf, Minister, the fatted calf.

HAWKINS. "On these conditions—"

RICHARD. The devil! Are there conditions?

HAWKINS. "To wit: first, that he shall not let my brother Peter's natural child starve or be driven by want to an evil life."

RICHARD [*emphatically, striking his fist on the table*] Agreed.

Mrs Dudgeon, turning to look malignantly at Essie, misses her and looks quickly round to see where she has moved to; then, seeing that she has left the room without leave, closes her lips vengefully.

HAWKINS. "Second, that he shall be a good friend to my old horse Jim"—[*again shaking his head*] he should have written James, sir.

RICHARD. James shall live in clover. Go on.

HAWKINS.—"and keep my deaf farm labourer Prodger Feston in his service."

RICHARD. Prodger Feston shall get drunk every Saturday.

HAWKINS. "Third, that he make Christy a present on his marriage out of the ornaments in the best room."

RICHARD [*holding up the stuffed birds*] Here you are, Christy.

CHRISTY [*disappointed*] I'd rather have the china peacocks.

RICHARD. You shall have both. [*Christy is greatly pleased*]. Go on.

HAWKINS. "Fourthly and lastly, that he try to live at peace with his mother as far as she will consent to it."

RICHARD [*dubiously*] Hm! Anything more, Mr Hawkins?

HAWKINS [*solemnly*] "Finally I give and bequeath my soul into my Maker's hands, humbly asking forgiveness for all my sins and mistakes, and hoping that He will so guide my son that it may not be said that I have done wrong in trusting to him rather than to others in the perplexity of my last hour in this strange place."

ANDERSON. Amen.

THE UNCLES AND AUNTS. Amen.

RICHARD. My mother does not say Amen.

MRS DUDGEON [*rising, unable to give up her property without a struggle*] Mr Hawkins: is that a proper will? Remember, I have his rightful, legal will, drawn up by yourself, leaving all to me.

HAWKINS. This is a very wrongly and irregularly worded will, Mrs Dudgeon: though [*turning politely to Richard*] it contains in my judgment an excellent disposal of his property.

ANDERSON [*interposing before Mrs Dudgeon can retort*] That is not what you are asked, Mr Hawkins. Is it a legal will?

HAWKINS. The courts will sustain it against the other.

ANDERSON. But why, if the other is more lawfully worded?

HAWKINS. Because, sir, the courts will sustain the claim of a man—and that man the eldest son—against any woman, if they can. I warned you, Mrs Dudgeon, when you got me to draw that other will, that it was not a wise will, and that though you might make him sign it, he would never be easy until he revoked it. But you wouldnt take advice; and now Mr Richard is cock of the walk. [*He takes his hat from the floor; rises; and begins pocketing his papers and spectacles*].

This is the signal for the breaking-up of the party. Anderson takes his hat from the rack and joins Uncle William at the fire. Titus fetches Judith her things from the rack. The three on the sofa rise and chat with Hawkins. Mrs Dudgeon, now an intruder in her own house, stands inert, crushed by the weight of the law on women, accepting it, as she has been trained to accept all monstrous calamities, as proofs of the greatness of the power that inflicts them, and of her own worm-like insignificance. For at this time, remember, Mary Wollstonecraft is as yet only a girl of eighteen, and her Vindication of the Rights of

Women is still fourteen years off. Mrs Dudgeon is rescued from her apathy by Essie, who comes back with the jug full of water. She is taking it to Richard when Mrs Dudgeon stops her.

MRS DUDGEON [*threatening her*] Where have you been? [*Essie, appalled, tries to answer, but cannot*]. How dare you go out by yourself after the orders I gave you?

ESSIE. He asked for a drink—[*she stops, her tongue cleaving to her palate with terror*].

JUDITH [*with gentler severity*] Who asked for a drink? [*Essie, speechless, points to Richard*].

RICHARD. What! I!

JUDITH [*shocked*] Oh Essie, Essie!

RICHARD. I believe I did. [*He takes a glass and holds it to Essie to be filled. Her hand shakes*]. What! afraid of me?

ESSIE [*quickly*] No. I—[*She pours out the water*].

RICHARD [*tasting it*] Ah, youve been up the street to the market gate spring to get that. [*He takes a draught*]. Delicious! Thank you. [*Unfortunately, at this moment he chances to catch sight of Judith's face, which expresses the most prudish disapproval of his evident attraction for Essie, who is devouring him with her grateful eyes. His mocking expression returns instantly. He puts down the glass; deliberately winds his arm round Essie's shoulders; and brings her into the middle of the company. Mrs Dudgeon being in Essie's way as they come past the table, he says*] By your leave, mother [*and compels her to make way for them*]. What do they call you? Bessie?

ESSIE. Essie.

RICHARD. Essie, to be sure. Are you a good girl, Essie?

ESSIE [*greatly disappointed that he, of all people, should begin at her in this way*] Yes. [*She looks doubtfully at Judith*]. I think so. I mean I—I hope so.

RICHARD. Essie: did you ever hear of a person called the devil?

ANDERSON [*revolted*] Shame on you, sir, with a mere child—

RICHARD. By your leave, Minister: I do not interfere with your sermons: do not you interrupt mine. [*To Essie*] Do you know what they call me, Essie?

ESSIE. Dick.

RICHARD [*amused: patting her on the shoulder*] Yes, Dick; but something else too. They call me the Devil's Disciple.

ESSIE. Why do you let them?

RICHARD [*seriously*] Because it's true. I was brought up in the other service; but I knew from the first that the Devil was my natural master and captain and friend. I saw that he was in the right, and that the world cringed to his conqueror only through fear. I prayed secretly to him: and he comforted me, and saved me from having my spirit broken in this house of children's tears. I promised him my soul, and swore an oath that I would stand up for him in this world and stand by him in the next. [*Solemnly*] That promise and that oath made a man of me. From this day this house is his home; and no child shall cry in it: this hearth is his altar; and no soul shall ever cower over it in the dark evenings and be afraid. Now [*turning forcibly on the rest*] which of you good men will take this child and rescue her from the house of the devil?

JUDITH [*coming to Essie and throwing a protecting arm about her*] I will. You should be burnt alive.

ESSIE. But I dont want to. [*She shrinks back, leaving Richard and Judith face to face*].

RICHARD [*to Judith*] Actually doesnt want to, most virtuous lady!

UNCLE TITUS. Have a care, Richard Dudgeon. The law—

RICHARD [*turning threateningly on him*] Have a care, you. In an hour from this there will be no law here but martial law. I passed the soldiers within six miles on my way here: before noon Major Swindon's gallows for rebels will be up in the market place.

ANDERSON [*calmly*] What have we to fear from that, sir?

RICHARD. More than you think. He hanged the wrong man at Springtown: he thought Uncle Peter was respectable, because the Dudgeons had a good name. But his next example will be the best man in the town to whom he can bring home a rebellious word. Well, we're all rebels; and you know it.

ALL THE MEN [*except Anderson*] No, no, no!

RICHARD. Yes, you are. You havnt damned King George up hill and down dale as I have; but youve prayed for his defeat; and you, Anthony Anderson, have conducted the service, and sold your family bible to buy a pair of pistols. They maynt hang me, perhaps; because the moral effect of the Devil's Disciple dancing on nothing wouldnt help them. But a minister! [*Judith, dismayed, clings to Anderson*] or a lawyer! [*Hawkins smiles like a man able to take care of himself*] or an upright horsedealer! [*Uncle Titus snarls at him in rage and terror*] or a reformed drunkard! [*Uncle William, utterly unnerved, moans and wobbles with fear*] eh? Would that shew that King George meant business—ha?

ANDERSON [*perfectly self-possessed*] Come, my dear: he is only trying to frighten you. There is no danger. [*He takes her out of the house. The rest crowd to the door to follow him, except Essie, who remains near Richard*].

RICHARD [*boisterously derisive*] Now then: how many of you will stay with me; run up the American flag on the devil's house; and make a fight for freedom? [*They scramble out, Christy among them, hustling one another in their haste*] Ha ha! Long live the devil! [*To Mrs Dudgeon, who is following them*] What, mother! Are you off too?

MRS DUDGEON [*deadly pale, with her hand on her heart as if she had received a deathblow*] My curse on you! My dying curse! [*She goes out*].

RICHARD [*calling after her*] It will bring me luck. Ha ha ha!

ESSIE [*anxiously*] Maynt I stay?

RICHARD [*turning to her*] What! Have they forgotten to save your soul in their anxiety about their own bodies? Oh yes: you may stay. [*He turns excitedly away again and shakes his fist after them. His left fist, also clenched, hangs down. Essie seizes it and kisses it, her tears falling on it. He starts and looks at it*]. Tears! The devil's baptism! [*She falls on her knees, sobbing. He stoops goodnaturedly to raise her, saying*] Oh yes, you may cry that way, Essie, if you like.

ACT II

Minister Anderson's house is in the main street of Webster-bridge, not far from the town hall. To the eye of the eighteenth century New Englander, it is much grander than the plain farmhouse of the Dudgeons; but it is so plain itself that a modern house agent would let both at about the same rent. The chief dwelling room has the same sort of kitchen fireplace, with boiler, toaster hanging on the bars, movable iron griddle socketed to the hob, hook above for roasting, and broad fender, on which stand a kettle and a plate of buttered toast. The door, between the fireplace and the corner, has neither panels, fingerplates nor handles: it is made of plain boards, and fastens with a latch. The table is a kitchen table, with a treacle colored cover of American cloth, chapped at the corners by draping. The tea service on it consists of two thick cups and saucers of the plainest ware, with milk jug and bowl to match, each large enough to contain nearly a quart, on a black japanned tray, and, in the middle of the table, a wooden trencher with a big loaf upon it, and a square half pound block of butter in a crock. The big oak press facing the fire from the opposite side of the room, is for use and storage, not for ornament; and the minister's house coat hangs on a peg from its door, shewing that he is out; for when he is in, it is his best coat that hangs there. His big riding boots stand beside the press, evidently in their usual place, and rather proud of themselves. In fact, the evolution of the minister's kitchen, dining room and drawing room into three separate apartments has not yet taken place; and so, from the point of view of our pampered period, he is no better off than the Dudgeons.

But there is a difference, for all that. To begin with, Mrs Anderson is a pleasanter person to live with than Mrs Dudgeon. To which Mrs Dudgeon would at once reply, with reason, that Mrs Anderson has no children to look after; no poultry, pigs nor cattle; a steady and sufficient income not directly dependent on harvests and prices at fairs; an affectionate husband who is a tower of strength to her: in short, that life is as easy at the minister's house as it is hard at the farm. This is true; but to explain a fact is not to alter it; and however little credit Mrs Anderson may deserve for making her home happier, she has certainly succeeded in doing it. The outward and visible signs of her superior social pretensions are, a drugget on the floor, a plaster ceiling between the timbers, and chairs which, though not upholstered, are stained and polished. The fine arts are represented by a mezzotint portrait of some Presbyterian divine, a copperplate of Raphael's St Paul preaching at Athens, a rococo presentation clock on the mantel-shelf, flanked by a couple of miniatures, a pair of crockery dogs with baskets in their mouths, and, at the corners, two large cowrie shells. A pretty feature of the room is the low wide latticed window, nearly its whole width, with little red curtains running on a rod half way up it to serve as a blind. There is no sofa; but one of the seats, standing near the press, has a railed back and is long enough to accommodate two people easily. On the whole, it is rather the sort of room that the nineteenth century has ended in struggling to get back to under the leadership of Mr Philip Webb and his disciples in domestic archi-tecture, though no genteel clergyman would have tolerated it fifty years ago.

The evening has closed in; and the room is dark except for the cosy firelight and the dim oil lamps seen through the window in the wet street where there is a quiet, steady, warm, windless downpour of rain. As the town clock strikes the quarter, Judith comes in with a couple of candles in earthenware candlesticks, and sets them on the table. Her self-conscious airs of the morning are gone: she is anxious and frightened. She goes to the window and peers into the street. The first thing she sees there is her husband, hurrying home through the rain. She gives a little gasp of relief, not very far removed from a sob, and turns to the door. Anderson comes in, wrapped in a very wet cloak.

JUDITH [*running to him*] Oh, here you are at last, at last! [*She attempts to embrace him*].

ANDERSON [*keeping her off*] Take care, my love: I'm wet. Wait till I get my cloak off. [*He places a chair with its back to the fire;*

hangs his cloak on it to dry; shakes the rain from his hat and puts it on the fender; and at last turns with his hands outstretched to Judith]. Now! [*She flies into his arms*]. I am not late, am I? The town clock struck the quarter as I came in at the front door. And the town clock is always fast.

JUDITH. I'm sure it's slow this evening. I'm so glad youre back.

ANDERSON [*taking her more closely in his arms*] Anxious, my dear?

JUDITH. A little.

ANDERSON. Why, youve been crying.

JUDITH. Only a little. Never mind: it's all over now. [*A bugle call is heard in the distance. She starts in terror and retreats to the long seat, listening.*] Whats that?

ANDERSON [*following her tenderly to the seat and making her sit down with him*] Only King George, my dear. He's returning to barracks, or having his roll called, or getting ready for tea, or booting or saddling or something. Soldiers dont ring the bell or call over the banisters when they want anything: they send a boy out with a bugle to disturb the whole town.

JUDITH. Do you think there is really any danger?

ANDERSON. Not the least in the world.

JUDITH. You say that to comfort me, not because you believe it.

ANDERSON. My dear: in this world there is always danger for those who are afraid of it. Theres a danger that the house will catch fire in the night; but we shant sleep any the less soundly for that.

JUDITH. Yes, I know what you always say; and youre quite right. Oh, quite right: I know it. But—I suppose I'm not brave: thats all. My heart shrinks every time I think of the soldiers.

ANDERSON. Never mind that, dear: bravery is none the worse for costing a little pain.

JUDITH. Yes, I suppose so, [*Embracing him again*] Oh how brave you are, my dear! [*With tears in her eyes*] Well, I'll be brave too: you shant be ashamed of your wife.

ANDERSON. Thats right. Now you make me happy. Well, well!

[*He rises and goes cheerily to the fire to dry his shoes*]. I called on Richard Dudgeon on my way back; but he wasnt in.

JUDITH [*rising in consternation*] You called on that man!

ANDERSON [*reassuring her*] Oh, nothing happened, dearie. He was out.

JUDITH [*almost in tears, as if the visit were a personal humiliation to her*] But why did you go there?

ANDERSON [*gravely*] Well, it is all the talk that Major Swindon is going to do what he did in Springtown—make an example of some notorious rebel, as he calls us. He pounced on Peter Dudgeon as the worst character there; and it is the general belief that he will pounce on Richard as the worst here.

JUDITH. But Richard said—

ANDERSON [*goodhumoredly cutting her short*] Pooh! Richard said! He said what he thought would frighten you and frighten me, my dear. He said what perhaps (God forgive him!) he would like to believe. It's a terrible thing to think of what death must mean for a man like that. I felt that I must warn him. I left a message for him.

JUDITH [*querulously*] What message?

ANDERSON. Only that I should be glad to see him for a moment on a matter of importance to himself, and that if he would look in here when he was passing he would be welcome.

JUDITH [*aghast*] You asked that man to come here!

ANDERSON. I did.

JUDITH [*sinking on the seat and clasping her hands*] I hope he wont come! Oh, I pray that he may not come!

ANDERSON. Why? Dont you want him to be warned?

JUDITH. He must know his danger. Oh, Tony, is it wrong to hate a blasphemer and a villain? I do hate him. I cant get him out of my mind: I know he will bring harm with him. He insulted you: he insulted me: he insulted his mother.

ANDERSON [*quaintly*] Well, dear, lets forgive him; and then it wont matter.

JUDITH. Oh, I know it's wrong to hate anybody; but—

ANDERSON [*going over to her with humorous tenderness*] Come, dear, youre not so wicked as you think. The worst sin towards our fellow creatures is not to hate them, but to be indifferent to them; thats the essence of inhumanity. After all, my dear, if you watch people carefully, youll be surprised to find how like hate is to love. [*She starts, strangely touched—even appalled. He is amused at her*]. Yes: I'm quite in earnest. Think of how some of our married friends worry one another, tax one another, are jealous of one another, cant bear to let one another out of sight for a day, are more like jailers and slave-owners than lovers. Think of those very same people with their enemies, scrupulous, lofty, self-respecting, determined to be independent of one another, careful of how they speak of one another—pooh! havnt you often thought that if they only knew it, they were better friends to their enemies than to their own husbands and wives? Come: depend on it, my dear, you are really fonder of Richard than you are of me, if you only knew it. Eh ?

JUDITH. Oh, dont say that: dont say that, Tony, even in jest. You dont know what a horrible feeling it gives me.

ANDERSON [*laughing*] Well, well: never mind, pet. He's a bad man; and you hate him as he deserves. And youre going to make the tea, arnt you?

JUDITH [*remorsefully*] Oh yes, I forgot. Ive been keeping you waiting all this time. [*She goes to the fire and puts on the kettle*].

ANDERSON [*going to the press and taking his coat off*] Have you stitched up the shoulder of my old coat?

JUDITH. Yes, dear. [*She goes to the table, and sets about putting the tea into the teapot from the caddy*].

ANDERSON [*as he changes his coat for the older one hanging on the press, and replaces it by the one he has just taken off*] Did anyone call when I was out?

JUDITH. No, only—[*Someone knocks at the door. With a start which betrays her intense nervousness, she retreats to the farther end of the table with the tea caddy and spoon in her hands exclaiming*] Who's that?

ANDERSON [*going to her and patting her encouragingly on the shoulder*] All right, pet, all right. He wont eat you, whoever he is. [*She tries to smile, and nearly makes herself cry. He goes to the door and opens it. Richard is there, without overcoat or cloak*]. You might have raised the latch and come in, Mr Dudgeon. Nobody stands on much ceremony with us. [*Hospitably*] Come in. [*Richard comes in carelessly and stands at the table, looking round the room with a slight pucker of his nose at the mezzotinted divine on the wall. Judith keeps her eyes on the tea caddy*]. Is it still raining? [*He shuts the door*].

RICHARD. Raining like the very [*his eye catches Judith's as she looks quickly and haughtily up*]—I beg your pardon; but [*shewing that his coat is wet*] you see—!

ANDERSON. Take it off, sir; and let it hang before the fire a while: my wife will excuse your shirtsleeves. Judith: put in another spoonful of tea for Mr Dudgeon.

RICHARD [*eyeing him cynically*] The magic of property, Pastor! Are even you civil to me now that I have succeeded to my father's estate?

Judith throws down the spoon indignantly.

ANDERSON [*quite unruffled, and helping Richard off with his coat*] I think, sir, that since you accept my hospitality, you cannot have so bad an opinion of it. Sit down. [*With the coat in his hand, he points to the railed seat. Richard, in his shirtsleeves, looks at him half quarrelsomely for a moment; then, with a nod, acknowledges that the minister has got the better of him, and sits down on the seat. Anderson pushes his cloak into a heap on the seat of the chair at the fire, and hangs Richard's coat on the back in its place*].

RICHARD. I come, sir, on your own invitation. You left word you had something important to tell me.

ANDERSON. I have a warning which it is my duty to give you.

RICHARD [*quickly rising*] You want to preach to me. Excuse me: I prefer a walk in the rain [*he makes for his coat*].

ANDERSON [*stopping him*] Dont be alarmed, sir: I am no great preacher. You are quite safe. [*Richard smiles in spite of himself. His glance softens: he even makes a gesture of excuse. Anderson, seeing that he has tamed him, now addresses him earnestly*] Mr Dudgeon: you are in danger in this town.

RICHARD. What danger?

ANDERSON. Your uncle's danger. Major Swindon's gallows.

RICHARD. It is you who are in danger. I warned you—

ANDERSON [*interrupting him goodhumoredly but authoritatively*] Yes, yes, Mr Dudgeon; but they do not think so in the town. And even if I were in danger, I have duties here which I must not forsake. But you are a free man. Why should you run any risk?

RICHARD. Do you think I should be any great loss, Minister?

ANDERSON. I think that a man's life is worth saving, whoever it belongs to. [*Richard makes him an ironical bow. Anderson returns the bow humorously*] Come: youll have a cup of tea, to prevent you catching cold?

RICHARD. I observe that Mrs Anderson is not quite so pressing as you are, Pastor.

JUDITH [*almost stifled with resentment, which she has been expecting her husband to share and express for her at every insult of Richard's*] You are welcome for my husband's sake. [*She brings the teapot to the fireplace and sets it on the hob*].

RICHARD. I know I am not welcome for my own, madam. [*He rises*]. But I think I will not break bread here, Minister.

ANDERSON [*cheerily*] Give me a good reason for that.

RICHARD. Because there is something in you that I respect, and that makes me desire to have you for my enemy.

ANDERSON. Thats well said. On these terms, sir, I will accept your enmity or any man's. Judith: Mr Dudgeon will stay to tea. Sit down: it will take a few minutes to draw by the fire. [*Richard glances at him with a troubled face; then sits down with his head bent, to hide a convulsive swelling of his throat*]. I was just saying to my wife, Mr Dudgeon, that enmity—[*She grasps his hand and looks imploringly at him, doing both with an intensity that checks him at once*]. Well, well, I mustnt tell you, I see; but it was nothing that need leave us worse friend—enemies, I mean. Judith is a great enemy of yours.

RICHARD. If all my enemies were like Mrs Anderson, I should be the best Christian in America.

ANDERSON [*gratified, patting her hand*] You hear that, Judith? Mr Dudgeon knows how to turn a compliment.

The latch is lifted from without.

JUDITH [*staring*] Who is that?

Christy comes in.

CHRISTY [*stopping and staring at Richard*] Oh, are you here?

RICHARD. Yes. Begone, you fool: Mrs Anderson doesnt want the whole family to tea at once.

CHRISTY [*coming further in*] Mother's very ill.

RICHARD. Well, does she want to see me?

CHRISTY. No.

RICHARD. I thought not.

CHRISTY. She wants to see the minister—at once.

JUDITH [*to Anderson*] Oh, not before youve had some tea.

ANDERSON. I shall enjoy it more when I come back, dear. [*He is about to take up his cloak*].

CHRISTY. The rain's over.

ANDERSON [*dropping the cloak and picking up his hat from the fender*] Where is your mother, Christy?

CHRISTY. At Uncle Titus's.

ANDERSON. Have you fetched the doctor?

CHRISTY. No: she didnt tell me to.

ANDERSON. Go on there at once: I'll overtake you on his doorstep. [*Christy turns to go*]. Wait a moment. Your brother must be anxious to know the particulars.

RICHARD. Psha! not I: he doesnt know; and I dont care. [*Violently*] Be off, you oaf. [*Christy runs out. Richard adds, a little shamefacedly*] We shall know soon enough.

ANDERSON. Well, perhaps you will let me bring you the news myself. Judith: will you give Mr Dudgeon his tea, and keep him here until I return.

JUDITH [*white and trembling*] Must I—

ANDERSON [*taking her hands and interrupting her to cover her agitation*] My dear: I can depend on you?

JUDITH [*with a piteous effort to be worthy of his trust*] Yes.

ANDERSON [*pressing her hand against his cheek*] You will not mind two old people like us, Mr Dudgeon. [*Going*] I shall not say good evening: you will be here when I come back. [*He goes out*].

They watch him pass the window, and then look at each other dumbly, quite disconcerted. Richard, noting the quiver of her lips, is the first to pull himself together.

RICHARD. Mrs Anderson: I am perfectly aware of the nature of your sentiments towards me. I shall not intrude on you. Good evening. [*Again he starts for the fireplace to get his coat*].

JUDITH [*getting between him and the coat*] No, no. Dont go: please dont go.

RICHARD [*roughly*] Why? You dont want me here.

JUDITH. Yes, I—[*Wringing her hands in despair*] Oh, if I tell you the truth, you will use it to torment me.

RICHARD [*indignantly*] Torment! What right have you to say that? Do you expect me to stay after that?

JUDITH. I want you to stay; but [*suddenly raging at him like an angry child*] it is not because I like you.

RICHARD. Indeed!

JUDITH. Yes: I had rather you did go than mistake me about that. I hate and dread you; and my husband knows it. If you are not here when he comes back, he will believe that I disobeyed him and drove you away.

RICHARD [*ironically*] Whereas, of course, you have really been so kind and hospitable and charming to me that I only want to go away out of mere contrariness, eh?

Judith, unable to bear it, sinks on the chair and bursts into tears.

RICHARD. Stop, stop, stop, I tell you. Dont do that. [*Putting his hand to his breast as if to a wound*] He wrung my heart by being a man. Need you tear it by being a woman? Has he not raised you

55

above my insults, like himself? [*She stops crying, and recovers herself somewhat, looking at him with a scared curiosity*]. There: thats right. [*Sympathetically*] Youre better now, arnt you? [*He puts his hand encouragingly on her shoulder. She instantly rises haughtily, and stares at him defiantly. He at once drops into his usual sardonic tone*]. Ah, thats better. You are yourself again: so is Richard. Well, shall we go to tea like a quiet respectable couple, and wait for your husband's return?

JUDITH [*rather ashamed of herself*] If you please. I—I am sorry to have been so foolish. [*She stoops to take up the plate of toast from the fender*].

RICHARD. I am sorry, for your sake, that I am—what I am. Allow me. [*He takes the plate from her and goes with it to the table*].

JUDITH [*following with the teapot*] Will you sit down? [*He sits down at the end of the table nearest the press. There is a plate and knife laid there. The other plate is laid near it: but Judith stays at the opposite end of the table, next the fire, and takes her place there, drawing the tray towards her*]. Do you take sugar?

RICHARD. No: but plenty of milk. Let me give you some toast. [*He puts some on the second plate, and hands it to her, with the knife. The action shews quickly how well he knows that she has avoided her usual place so as to be as far from him as possible*].

JUDITH [*consciously*] Thanks. [*She gives him his tea*]. Wont you help yourself?

RICHARD. Thanks. [*He puts a piece of toast on his own plate; and she pours out tea for herself*].

JUDITH [*observing that he tastes nothing*] Dont you like it? You are not eating anything.

RICHARD. Neither are you.

JUDITH [*nervously*] I never care much for my tea. Please dont mind me.

RICHARD [*looking dreamily round*] I am thinking. It is all so strange to me. I can see the beauty and peace of this home: I think I have never been more at rest in my life than at this moment; and yet I know quite well I could never live here. It's not in my nature, I suppose, to be domesticated. But it's very beautiful: it's almost holy. [*He muses a moment, and then laughs softly*].

JUDITH [*quickly*] Why do you laugh?

RICHARD. I was thinking that if any stranger came in here now, he would take us for man and wife.

JUDITH [*taking offence*] You mean, I suppose, that you are more my age than he is.

RICHARD [*staring at this unexpected turn*] I never thought of such a thing. [*Sardonic again*]. I see there is another side to domestic joy.

JUDITH [*angrily*] I would rather have a husband whom everybody respects than—than—

RICHARD. Than the devil's disciple. You are right; but I daresay your love helps him to be a good man, just as your hate helps me to be a bad one.

JUDITH. My husband has been very good to you. He has forgiven you for insulting him, and is trying to save you. Can you not forgive him for being so much better than you are? How dare you belittle him by putting yourself in his place?

RICHARD. Did I?

JUDITH. Yes, you did. You said that if anybody came in they would take us for man and—[*She stops, terrorstricken, as a squad of soldiers tramps past the window*]. The English soldiers! Oh, what do they—

RICHARD [*listening*] Sh!

A VOICE [*outside*] Halt! Four outside: two in with me.

Judith half rises, listening and looking with dilated eyes at Richard, who takes up his cup prosaically, and is drinking his tea when the latch goes up with a sharp click, and an English sergeant walks into the room with two privates, who post themselves at the door. He comes promptly to the table between them.

THE SERGEANT. Sorry to disturb you, mum. Duty! Anthony Anderson: I arrest you in King George's name as a rebel.

JUDITH [*pointing at Richard*] But that is not—[*He looks up quickly at her, with a face of iron. She stops her mouth hastily with the hand she has raised to indicate him, and stands staring affrightedly*].

THE SERGEANT. Come, parson: put your coat on and come along.

RICHARD. Yes: I'll come. [*He rises and takes a step towards his own coat; then recollects himself, and, with his back to the sergeant, moves his gaze slowly round the room without turning his head until he sees Anderson's black coat hanging up on the press. He goes composedly to it; takes it down; and puts it on. The idea of himself as a parson tickles him: he looks down at the black sleeve on his arm, and then smiles slyly at Judith, whose white face shews him that what she is painfully struggling to grasp is not the humor of the situation but its horror. He turns to the sergeant, who is approaching him with a pair of handcuffs hidden behind him, and says lightly*] Did you ever arrest a man of my cloth before, Sergeant?

THE SERGEANT [*instinctively respectful, half to the black coat, and half to Richard's good breeding*] Well, no sir. At least, only an army chaplain. [*Shewing the handcuffs*]. I'm sorry sir; but duty—

RICHARD. Just so, Sergeant. Well, I'm not ashamed of them: thank you kindly for the apology. [*He holds out his hands*].

SERGEANT [*not availing himself of the offer*] One gentleman to another, sir. Wouldnt you like to say a word to your missis, sir, before you go?

RICHARD [*smiling*] Oh, we shall meet again before—eh? [*meaning "before you hang me"*].

SERGEANT [*loudly, with ostentatious cheerfulness*] Oh, of course, of course. No call for the lady to distress herself. Still—[*in a lower voice, intended for Richard alone*] your last chance, sir.

They look at one another significantly for a moment. Then Richard exhales a deep breath and turns towards Judith.

RICHARD [*very distinctly*] My love. [*She looks at him, pitiably pale, and tries to answer, but cannot—tries also to come to him, but cannot trust herself to stand without the support of the table*]. This gallant gentleman is good enough to allow us a moment of leave-taking. [*The sergeant retires delicately and joins his men near the door*]. He is trying to spare you the truth; but you had better know it. Are you listening to me? [*She signifies assent*]. Do you understand that I am going to my death? [*She signifies that she understands*]. Remember, you must find our friend who was with us just now. Do you understand? [*She signifies yes*]. See that you get him safely out of harm's way. Dont for your life let him know of my danger; but if he finds it out, tell him that he cannot save me: they would hang him; and they would not spare me. And tell him that I am steadfast in my religion as he is in his, and that he may depend on me to the death. [*He turns to go, and meets the eyes of the sergeant, who looks a little suspicious. He considers a moment, and then, turning roguishly to Judith with something of a smile breaking through his earnestness, says*] And now, my dear, I am afraid the sergeant will not believe that you love me like a wife unless you give one kiss before I go.

He approaches her and holds out his arms. She quits the table and almost falls into them.

JUDITH [*the words choking her*] I ought to—it's murder—

RICHARD. No: only a kiss [*softly to her*] for his sake.

JUDITH. I cant. You must—

RICHARD [*folding her in his arms with an impulse of compassion for her distress*] My poor girl!

Judith, with a sudden effort, throws her arms round him; kisses him; and swoons away, dropping from his arms to the ground as if the kiss had killed her.

RICHARD [*going quickly to the sergeant*] Now, Sergeant: quick, before she comes to. The handcuffs. [*He puts out his hands*].

SERGEANT [*pocketing them*] Never mind, sir: I'll trust you. Youre a game one. You ought to a bin a soldier, sir. Between them two, please. [*The soldiers place themselves one before Richard and one behind him. The sergeant opens the door*].

RICHARD [*taking a last look round him*] Goodbye, wife: goodbye, home. Muffle the drums, and quick march!

The sergeant signs to the leading soldier to march. They file out quickly. * * * * * * * * * * * * * * * *When Anderson returns from*

Mrs Dudgeon's, he is astonished to find the room apparently empty and almost in darkness except for the glow from the fire; for one of the candles has burnt out, and the other is at its last flicker.

ANDERSON. Why, what on earth—? [*Calling*] Judith, Judith! [*He listens: there is no answer*]. Hm! [*He goes to the cupboard; takes a candle from the drawer; lights it at the flicker of the expiring one on the table; and looks wonderingly at the untasted meal by its light. Then he sticks it in the candlestick; takes off his hat; and scratches his head, much puzzled. This action causes him to look at the floor for the first time; and there he sees Judith lying motionless with her eyes closed. He runs to her and stoops beside her, lifting her head*]. Judith.

JUDITH [*waking; for her swoon has passed into the sleep of exhaustion after suffering*] Yes. Did you call? Whats the matter?

ANDERSON. Ive just come in and found you lying here with the candles burnt out and the tea poured out and cold. What has happened?

JUDITH [*still astray*] I dont know. Have I been asleep? I suppose — [*She stops blankly*], I dont know.

ANDERSON [*groaning*] Heaven forgive me, I left you alone with that scoundrel. [*Judith remembers. With an agonized cry, she clutches his shoulders and drags herself to her feet as he rises with her. He clasps her tenderly in his arms*]. My poor pet!

JUDITH [*frantically clinging to him*] What shall I do? Oh my God, what shall I do?

ANDERSON. Never mind, never mind, my dearest dear: it was my fault. Come: youre safe now; and youre not hurt, are you? [*He takes his arms from her to see whether she can stand*]. There: thats right, thats right. If only you are not hurt, nothing else matters.

JUDITH. No, no, no: I'm not hurt.

ANDERSON. Thank Heaven for that! Come now: [*leading her to the railed seat and making her sit down beside him*] sit down and rest: you can tell me about it tomorrow. Or [*misunderstanding her distress*] you shall not tell me at all if it worries you. There, there!

[*Cheerfully*] I'll make you some fresh tea: that will set you up again. [*He goes to the table, and empties the teapot into the slop bowl*].

JUDITH [*in a strained tone*] Tony.

ANDERSON. Yes, dear?

JUDITH. Do you think we are only in a dream now?

ANDERSON [*glancing round at her for a moment with a pang of anxiety, though he goes on steadily and cheerfully putting fresh tea into the pot*] Perhaps so, pet. But you may as well dream a cup of tea when youre about it.

JUDITH. Oh stop, stop. You dont know— [*Distracted, she buries her face in her knotted hands*].

ANDERSON [*breaking down and coming to her*] My dear, what is it? I cant bear it any longer: you must tell me. It was all my fault: I was mad to trust him.

JUDITH. No: dont say that. You mustnt say that. He—oh no, no: I cant. Tony: dont speak to me. Take my hands—both my hands. [*He takes them, wondering*]. Make me think of you, not of him. Theres danger, frightful danger; but it is your danger; and I cant keep thinking of it: I cant, I cant: my mind goes back to his danger. He must be saved—no: you must be saved: you, you, you. [*She springs up as if to do something or go somewhere, exclaiming*] Oh, Heaven help me?

ANDERSON [*keeping his seat and holding her hands with resolute composure*] Calmly, calmly, my pet. Youre quite distracted.

JUDITH. I may well be. I dont know what to do. I dont know what to do. [*Tearing her hands away*]. I must save him. [*Anderson rises in alarm as she runs wildly to the door. It is opened in her face by Essie, who hurries in full of anxiety. The surprise is so disagreeable to Judith that it brings her to her senses. Her tone is sharp and angry as she demands*] What do you want?

ESSIE. I was to come to you.

ANDERSON. Who told you to?

ESSIE [*staring at him, as if his presence astonished her*] Are you here?

61

JUDITH. Of course. Dont be foolish, child.

ANDERSON. Gently, dearest: youll frighten her. [*Going between them*]. Come here, Essie. [*She comes to him*]. Who sent you?

ESSIE. Dick. He sent me word by a soldier. I was to come here at once and do whatever Mrs Anderson told me.

ANDERSON [*enlightened*] A soldier! Ah, I see it all now! They have arrested Richard. [*Judith makes a gesture of despair*].

ESSIE. No. I asked the soldier. Dick's safe. But the soldier said you had been taken.

ANDERSON. I! [*Bewildered, he turns to Judith for an explanation*].

JUDITH [*coaxingly*] All right, dear: I understand. [*To Essie*] Thank you, Essie, for coming: but I dont need you now. You may go home.

ESSIE [*suspicious*] Are you sure Dick has not been touched? Perhaps he told the soldier to say it was the minister. [*Anxiously*] Mrs Anderson: do you think it can have been that?

ANDERSON. Tell her the truth if it is so, Judith. She will learn it from the first neighbor she meets in the street. [*Judith turns away and covers her eyes with her hands*].

ESSIE [*wailing*] But what will they do to him? Oh, what will they do to him? Will they hang him? [*Judith shudders convulsively, and throws herself into the chair in which Richard sat at the tea table*].

ANDERSON [*patting Essie's shoulder and trying to comfort her*] I hope not. I hope not. Perhaps if youre very quiet and patient, we may be able to help him in some way.

ESSIE. Yes—help him—yes, yes, yes. I'll be good.

ANDERSON. I must go to him at once, Judith.

JUDITH [*springing up*] Oh no. You must go away—far away, to some place of safety.

ANDERSON. Pooh!

JUDITH [*passionately*] Do you want to kill me? Do you think I can bear to live for days and days with every knock at the door—every footstep—giving me a spasm of terror? to lie awake for nights and nights in an agony of dread, listening for them to come and arrest you?

ANDERSON. Do you think it would be better to know that I had run away from my post at the first sign of danger?

JUDITH [*bitterly*] Oh, you wont go. I know it. Youll stay; and I shall go mad.

ANDERSON. My dear, your duty—

JUDITH [*fiercely*] What do I care about my duty?

ANDERSON [*shocked*] Judith!

JUDITH. I am doing my duty. I am clinging to my duty. My duty is to get you away, to save you, to leave him to his fate [*Essie utters a cry of distress and sinks on the chair at the fire, sobbing silently*]. My instinct is the same as hers—to save him above all things, though it would be so much better for him to die! so much greater! But I know you will take your own way as he took it. I have no power. [*She sits down sullenly on the railed seat*] I'm only a woman; I can do nothing but sit here and suffer. Only, tell him I tried to save you—that I did my best to save you.

ANDERSON. My dear, I am afraid he will be thinking more of his own danger than of mine.

JUDITH. Stop; or I shall hate you.

ANDERSON [*remonstrating*] Come, come, come! How am I to leave you if you talk like this? You are quite out of your senses. [*He turns to Essie*] Essie.

ESSIE [*eagerly rising and drying her eyes*] Yes?

ANDERSON. Just wait outside a moment, like a good girl; Mrs Anderson is not well. [*Essie looks doubtful*]. Never fear; I'll come to you presently; and I'll go to Dick.

ESSIE. You are sure you will go to him? [*Whispering*]. You wont let her prevent you?

ANDERSON [*smiling*] No, no; it's all right. All right. [*She goes*]. Thats a good girl. [*He closes the door, and returns to Judith*].

JUDITH [*seated—rigid*] You are going to your death.

ANDERSON [*quaintly*] Then I shall go in my best coat, dear. [*He turns to the press, beginning to take off his coat*]. Where—? [*He stares at the empty nail for a moment; then looks quickly round to the fire; strides across to it; and lifts Richard's coat*]. Why, my dear, it seems that he has gone in my best coat.

JUDITH [*still motionless*] Yes.

ANDERSON. Did the soldiers make a mistake?

JUDITH. Yes: they made a mistake.

ANDERSON. He might have told them. Poor fellow, he was too upset, I suppose.

JUDITH. Yes: he might have told them. So might I.

ANDERSON. Well, it's all very puzzling—almost funny. It's curious how these little things strike us even in the most—[*He breaks off and begins putting on Richard's coat*] I'd better take him his own coat. I know what he'll say—[*imitating Richard's sardonic manner*] "Anxious about my soul, Pastor, and also about your best coat." Eh?

JUDITH. Yes, that is just what he will say to you. [*Vacantly*] It doesnt matter: I shall never see either of you again.

ANDERSON [*rallying her*] Oh pooh, pooh, pooh! [*He sits down beside her*]. Is this how you keep your promise that I shant be ashamed of my brave wife?

JUDITH. No: this is how I break it. I cannot keep my promises to him: why should I keep my promises to you?

ANDERSON. Dont speak so strangely, my love. It sounds insincere to me. [*She looks unutterable reproach at him*]. Yes, dear, nonsense is always insincere; and my dearest is talking nonsense. Just nonsense. [*Her face darkens into dumb obstinacy. She stares straight before her, and does not look at him again, absorbed in Richard's fate. He scans her face; sees that his rallying has produced no effect; and gives it up, making no further effort to conceal his anxiety*]. I wish I knew what has frightened you so. Was there a struggle? Did he fight?

JUDITH. No. He smiled.

ANDERSON. Did he realize his danger, do you think?

JUDITH. He realized yours.

ANDERSON. Mine!

JUDITH [*monotonously*] He said "See that you get him safely out of harm's way." I promised: I cant keep my promise. He said, "Dont for your life let him know of my danger." Ive told you of it. He said that if you found it out, you could not save him—that they will hang him and not spare you.

ANDERSON [*rising in generous indignation*] And you think that I will let a man with that much good in him die like a dog, when a few words might make him die like a Christian. I'm ashamed of you, Judith.

JUDITH. He will be steadfast in his religion as you are in yours; and you may depend on him to the death. He said so.

ANDERSON. God forgive him! What else did he say?

JUDITH. He said goodbye.

ANDERSON [*fidgeting nervously to and fro in great concern*] Poor fellow, poor fellow! You said goodbye to him in all kindness and charity, Judith, I hope.

JUDITH. I kissed him.

ANDERSON. What! Judith!

JUDITH. Are you angry?

ANDERSON. No, no. You were right: you were right. Poor fellow, poor fellow! [*Greatly distressed*] To be hanged like that at his age! And then did they take him away?

JUDITH [*wearily*] Then you were here: thats the next thing I remember. I suppose I fainted. Now bid me goodbye, Tony. Perhaps I shall faint again. I wish I could die.

ANDERSON. No, no, my dear: you must pull yourself together and be sensible. I am in no danger—not the least in the world.

JUDITH [*solemnly*] You are going to your death, Tony—your sure death, if God will let innocent men be murdered. They will not let you see him: they will arrest you the moment you give your name. It was for you the soldiers came.

ANDERSON [*thunderstruck*] For me!!! [*His fists clinch; his neck thickens; his face reddens; the fleshy purses under his eyes become injected with hot blood; the man of peace vanishes, transfigured into a choleric and formidable man of war. Still, she does not come out of her absorption to look at him: her eyes are steadfast with a mechanical reflection of Richard's steadfastness*].

JUDITH. He took your place: he is dying to save you. That is why he went in your coat. That is why I kissed him.

ANDERSON [*exploding*] Blood an' owns! [*His voice is rough and dominant, his gesture full of brute energy*]. Here! Essie, Essie!

ESSIE [*running in*] Yes.

ANDERSON [*impetuously*] Off with you as hard as you can run, to the inn. Tell them to saddle the fastest and strongest horse they have [*Judith rises breathless, and stares at him incredulously*]—the chestnut mare, if she's fresh—without a moment's delay. Go into the stable yard and tell the black man there that I'll give him a silver dollar if the horse is waiting for me when I come, and that I am close on your heels. Away with you. [*His energy sends Essie flying from the room. He pounces on his riding boots; rushes with them to the chair at the fire; and begins pulling them on*].

JUDITH [*unable to believe such a thing of him*] You are not going to him!

ANDERSON [*busy with the boots*] Going to him! What good would that do? [*Growling to himself as he gets the first boot on with a wrench*] I'll go to them, so I will. [*To Judith peremptorily*] Get me the pistols: I want them. And money, money: I want money—all the money in the house. [*He stoops over the other boot, grumbling*] A great satisfaction it would be to him to have my company on the gallows. [*He pulls on the boot*].

JUDITH. You are deserting him, then?

ANDERSON. Hold your tongue, woman; and get me the pistols. [*She goes to the press and takes from it a leather belt with two pistols, a powder horn, and a bag of bullets attached to it. She throws it on the table. Then she unlocks a drawer in the press and takes out a purse. Anderson grabs the belt and buckles it on, saying*] If they took him for me in my coat, perhaps theyll take me for him in his. [*Hitching the belt into its place*] Do I look like him?

JUDITH [*turning with the purse in her hand*] Horribly unlike him.

ANDERSON [*snatching the purse from her and emptying it on the table*] Hm! We shall see.

JUDITH [*sitting down helplessly*] Is it of any use to pray, do you think, Tony?

ANDERSON [*counting the money*] Pray! Can we pray Swindon's rope off Richard's neck?

JUDITH. God may soften Major Swindon's heart.

ANDERSON [*contemptuously—pocketing a handful of money*] Let him, then. I am not God; and I must go to work another way. [*Judith gasps at the blasphemy. He throws the purse on the table*]. Keep that. Ive taken 25 dollars.

JUDITH. Have you forgotten even that you are a minister?

ANDERSON. Minister be—faugh! My hat: wheres my hat? [*He snatches up hat and cloak, and puts both on in hot haste*] Now listen, you. If you can get a word with him by pretending youre his wife, tell him to hold his tongue until morning: that will give me all the start I need.

JUDITH [*solemnly*] You may depend on him to the death.

ANDERSON. Youre a fool, a fool, Judith. [*For a moment checking the torrent of his haste, and speaking with something of his old quiet and impressive conviction*] You dont know the man youre married to. [*Essie returns. He swoops at her at once*]. Well: is the horse ready?

ESSIE [*breathless*] It will be ready when you come.

ANDERSON. Good. [*He makes for the door*].

JUDITH [*rising and stretching out her arms after him involuntarily*] Wont you say goodbye?

ANDERSON. And waste another half minute! Psha! [*He rushes out like an avalanche*].

ESSIE [*hurrying to Judith*] He has gone to save Richard, hasnt he?

JUDITH. To save Richard! No: Richard has saved him. He has gone to save himself. Richard must die.

Essie screams with terror and falls on her knees, hiding her face. Judith, without heeding her, looks rigidly straight in front of her, at the vision of Richard, dying.

ACT III

Early next morning the sergeant, at the British headquarters in the Town Hall, unlocks the door of a little empty panelled waiting room, and invites Judith to enter. She has had a bad night, probably a rather delirious one; for even in the reality of the raw morning, her fixed gaze comes back at moments when her attention is not strongly held.

The sergeant considers that her feelings do her credit, and is sympathetic in an encouraging military way. Being a fine figure of a man, vain of his uniform and of his rank, he feels specially qualified, in a respectful way, to console her.

SERGEANT. You can have a quiet word with him here, mum.

JUDITH. Shall I have long to wait?

SERGEANT. No, mum, not a minute. We kep him in the Bridewell for the night; and he's just been brought over here for the court martial. Dont fret, mum: he slep like a child, and has made a rare good breakfast.

JUDITH [*incredulously*] He is in good spirits!

SERGEANT. Tip top, mum. The chaplain looked in to see him last night; and he won seventeen shillings off him at spoil five. He spent it among us like the gentleman he is. Duty's duty, mum, of course; but youre among friends here. [*The tramp of a couple of soldiers is heard approaching*]. There: I think he's coming. [*Richard comes in, without a sign of care or captivity in his bearing. The sergeant nods to the two soldiers, and shows them the key of the room in his hand. They withdraw*]. Your good lady, sir.

RICHARD [*going to her*] What! My wife. My adored one. [*He takes her hand and kisses it with a perverse, raffish gallantry*]. How long do you allow a brokenhearted husband for leave-taking, Sergeant?

SERGEANT. As long as we can, sir. We shall not disturb you till the court sits.

RICHARD. But it has struck the hour.

SERGEANT. So it has, sir; but theres a delay. General Burgoyne's just arrived—Gentlemanly Johnny we call him, sir—and he wont have done finding fault with everything this side of half past. I know him, sir: I served with him in Portugal. You may count on twenty minutes, sir; and by your leave I wont waste any more of them. [*He goes out, locking the door. Richard immediately drops his raffish manner and turns to Judith with considerate sincerity*].

RICHARD. Mrs Anderson: this visit is very kind of you. And how are you after last night? I had to leave you before you recovered; but I sent word to Essie to go and look after you. Did she understand the message?

JUDITH [*breathless and urgent*] Oh, dont think of me: I havnt come here to talk about myself. Are they going to—to—[*meaning "to hang you"*]?

RICHARD [*whimsically*] At noon, punctually. At least, that was when they disposed of Uncle Peter. [*She shudders*]. Is your husband safe? Is he on the wing?

JUDITH. He is no longer my husband.

RICHARD [*opening his eyes wide*] Eh?

JUDITH. I disobeyed you. I told him everything. I expected him to come here and save you. I wanted him to come here and save you. He ran away instead.

RICHARD. Well, thats what I meant him to do. What good would his staying have done? Theyd only have hanged us both.

JUDITH [*with reproachful earnestness*] Richard Dudgeon: on your honor, what would you have done in his place?

RICHARD. Exactly what he has done, of course.

JUDITH. Oh, why will you not be simple with me—honest and straightforward? If you are so selfish as that, why did you let them take you last night?

RICHARD [*gaily*] Upon my life, Mrs Anderson, I dont know. Ive been asking myself that question ever since; and I can find no manner of reason for acting as I did.

JUDITH. You know you did it for his sake, believing he was a more worthy man than yourself.

RICHARD [*laughing*] Oho! No: thats a very pretty reason, I must say; but I'm not so modest as that. No: it wasnt for his sake.

JUDITH [*after a pause, during which she looks shamefacedly at him, blushing painfully*] Was it for my sake?

RICHARD [*gallantly*] Well, you had a hand in it. It must have been a little for your sake. You let them take me, at all events.

JUDITH. Oh, do you think I have not been telling myself that all night? Your death will be at my door. [*Impulsively, she gives him her hand, and adds, with intense earnestness*] If I could save you as you saved him, I would do it, no matter how cruel the death was.

RICHARD [*holding her hand and smiling, but keeping her almost at arms length*] I am very sure I shouldnt let you.

JUDITH. Dont you see that I can save you?

RICHARD. How? by changing clothes with me, eh?

JUDITH [*disengaging her hand to touch his lips with it*] Dont [*meaning "Dont jest"*]. No: by telling the court who you really are.

RICHARD [*frowning*] No use: they wouldnt spare me; and it would spoil half his chance of escaping. They are determined to cow us by making an example of somebody on that gallows to-day. Well, let us cow them by showing that we can stand by one another to the death. That is the only force that can send Burgoyne back across the Atlantic and make America a nation.

JUDITH [*impatiently*] Oh, what does all that matter?

RICHARD [*laughing*] True: what does it matter? what does anything matter? You see, men have these strange notions, Mrs Anderson; and women see the folly of them.

JUDITH. Women have to lose those they love through them.

RICHARD. They can easily get fresh lovers.

JUDITH [*revolted*] Oh! [*Vehemently*] Do you realize that you are going to kill yourself?

RICHARD. The only man I have any right to kill, Mrs Anderson. Dont be concerned: no woman will lose her lover through my death. [*Smiling*] Bless you, nobody cares for me. Have you heard that my mother is dead?

JUDITH. Dead!

RICHARD. Of heart disease—in the night. Her last word to me was her curse: I dont think I could have borne her blessing. My other relatives will not grieve much on my account. Essie will cry for a day or two; but I have provided for her: I made my own will last night.

JUDITH [*stonily, after a moment's silence*] And I!

RICHARD [*surprised*] You?

JUDITH. Yes, I. Am I not to care at all?

RICHARD [*gaily and bluntly*] Not a scrap. Oh, you expressed your feelings towards me very frankly yesterday. What happened may have softened you for the moment; but believe me, Mrs Anderson, you dont like a bone in my skin or a hair on my head. I shall be as good a riddance at 12 today as I should have been at 12 yesterday.

JUDITH [*her voice trembling*] What can I do to shew you that you are mistaken.

RICHARD. Dont trouble. I'll give you credit for liking me a little better than you did. All I say is that my death will not break your heart.

JUDITH [*almost in a whisper*] How do you know? [*She puts her hands on his shoulders and looks intently at him*].

RICHARD [*amazed—divining the truth*] Mrs Anderson! [*The bell of the town clock strikes the quarter. He collects himself, and removes her hands, saying rather coldly*] Excuse me: they will be here for me presently. It is too late.

JUDITH. It is not too late. Call me as witness: they will never kill you when they know how heroically you have acted.

RICHARD [*with some scorn*] Indeed! But if I dont go through with it, where will the heroism be? I shall simply have tricked them; and theyll hang me for that like a dog. Serve me right too!

JUDITH [*wildly*] Oh, I believe you want to die.

RICHARD [*obstinately*] No I dont.

JUDITH. Then why not try to save yourself? I implore you—listen. You said just now that you saved him for my sake—yes [*clutching him as he recoils with a gesture of denial*] a little for my sake. Well, save yourself for my sake. And I will go with you to the end of the world.

RICHARD [*taking her by the wrists and holding her a little way from him, looking steadily at her*] Judith.

JUDITH [*breathless—delighted at the name*] Yes.

RICHARD. If I said—to please you—that I did what I did ever so little for your sake, I lied as men always lie to women. You know how much I have lived with worthless men—aye, and worthless women too. Well, they could all rise to some sort of goodness and kindness when they were in love [*the word love comes from him with true Puritan scorn*]. That has taught me to set very little store by the goodness that only comes out red hot. What I did last night, I did in cold blood, caring not half so much for your husband, or [*ruthlessly*] for you [*she droops, stricken*] as I do for myself. I had no motive and no interest: all I can tell you is that when it came to the point whether I would take my neck out of the noose and put another man's into it, I would not do it. I dont know why not: I see myself as a fool for my pains; but I could not and I cannot. I have been brought up standing by the law of my own nature; and I may not go against it, gallows or no gallows. [*She has slowly raised her head and is now looking full at him*]. I should have done the same for any other man in the town, or any other man's wife. [*Releasing her*] Do you understand that?

JUDITH. Yes: you mean that you do not love me.

RICHARD [*revolted—with fierce contempt*] Is that all it means to you?

JUDITH. What more—what worse—can it mean to me? [*The sergeant knocks. The blow on the door jars on her heart*]. Oh, one moment more. [*She throws herself on her knees*]. I pray to you—

RICHARD. Hush! [*Calling*] Come in. [*The sergeant unlocks the door and opens it. The guard is with him*].

SERGEANT [*coming in*] Time's up, sir.

RICHARD. Quite ready, Sergeant. Now, my dear. [*He attempts to raise her*].

JUDITH [*clinging to him*] Only one thing more—I entreat, I implore you. Let me be present in the court. I have seen Major Swindon: he said I should be allowed if you asked it. You will ask it. It is my last request: I shall never ask you anything again. [*She clasps his knee*]. I beg and pray it of you.

RICHARD. If I do, will you be silent?

JUDITH. Yes.

RICHARD. You will keep faith?

JUDITH. I will keep—[*She breaks down, sobbing*].

RICHARD [*taking her arm to lift her*] Just—her other arm, Sergeant.

They go out, she sobbing convulsively, supported by the two men.

Meanwhile, the Council Chamber is ready for the court martial. It is a large, lofty room, with a chair of state in the middle under a tall canopy with a gilt crown, and maroon curtains with the royal monogram G.R. In front of the chair is a table, also draped in maroon, with a bell, a heavy inkstand, and writing materials on it. Several chairs are set at the table. The door is at the right hand of the occupant of the chair of state when it has an occupant: at present it is empty. Major Swindon, a pale, sandy-haired, very conscientious looking man of about 45, sits at the end of the table with his back to the door, writing. He is alone until the sergeant announces the General in a subdued manner which suggests that Gentlemanly Johnny has been making his presence felt rather heavily.

SERGEANT. The General, sir.

Swindon rises hastily. The general comes in: the sergeant goes out. General Burgoyne is 55, and very well preserved. He is a man of fashion, gallant enough to have made a distinguished marriage by an elopement, witty enough to write successful comedies, aristocratically-connected enough to have had opportunities of high military distinction. His eyes, large, brilliant, apprehensive, and intelligent, are his most remarkable feature: without them his fine nose and small mouth would suggest rather more fastidiousness and less force than go to the making of a first rate general. Just now the eyes are angry and tragic, and the mouth and the nostrils tense.

73

BURGOYNE. Major Swindon, I presume.

SWINDON. Yes. General Burgoyne, if I mistake not. [*They bow to one another ceremoniously*]. I am glad to have the support of your presence this morning. It is not particularly lively business, hanging this poor devil of a minister.

BURGOYNE [*throwing himself into Swindon's chair*] No, sir, it is not. It is making too much of the fellow to execute him: what more could you have done if he had been a member of the Church of England? Martyrdom, sir, is what these people like: it is the only way in which a man can become famous without ability. However, you have committed us to hanging him; and the sooner he is hanged the better.

SWINDON. We have arranged it for 12 o'clock. Nothing remains to be done except to try him.

BURGOYNE [*looking at him with suppressed anger*] Nothing— except to save your own necks, perhaps. Have you heard the news from Springtown?

SWINDON. Nothing special. The latest reports are satisfactory.

BURGOYNE [*rising in amazement*] Satisfactory, sir! Satisfactory!! [*He stares at him for a moment, and then adds, with grim intensity*] I am glad you take that view of them.

SWINDON [*puzzled*] Do I understand that in your opinion—

BURGOYNE. I do not express my opinion. I never stoop to that habit of profane language which unfortunately coarsens our profession. If I did, sir, perhaps I should be able to express my opinion of the news from Springtown—the news which you [*severely*] have apparently not heard. How soon do you get news from your supports here?—in the course of a month, eh?

SWINDON [*turning sulky*] I suppose the reports have been taken to you, sir, instead of to me. Is there anything serious?

BURGOYNE [*taking a report from his pocket and holding it up*] Springtown's in the hands of the rebels. [*He throws the report on the table*].

SWINDON [*aghast*] Since yesterday!

BURGOYNE. Since two o'clock this morning. Perhaps we shall

be in their hands before two o'clock tomorrow morning. Have you thought of that?

SWINDON [*confidently*] As to that, General, the British soldier will give a good account of himself.

BURGOYNE [*bitterly*] And therefore, I suppose, sir, the British officer need not know his business: the British soldier will get him out of all his blunders with the bayonet. In future, sir, I must ask you to be a little less generous with the blood of your men, and a little more generous with your own brains.

SWINDON. I am sorry I cannot pretend to your intellectual eminence, sir. I can only do my best, and rely on the devotion of my countrymen.

BURGOYNE [*suddenly becoming suavely sarcastic*] May I ask are you writing a melodrama, Major Swindon?

SWINDON [*flushing*] No, sir.

BURGOYNE. What a pity! What a pity! [*Dropping his sarcastic tone and facing him suddenly and seriously*] Do you at all realize, sir, that we have nothing standing between us and destruction but our own bluff and the sheepishness of these colonists? They are men of the same English stock as ourselves: six to one of us [*repeating it emphatically*] six to one, sir; and nearly half our troops are Hessians, Brunswickers, German dragoons, and Indians with scalping knives. These are the countrymen on whose devotion you rely! Suppose the colonists find a leader! Suppose the news from Springtown should turn out to mean that they have already found a leader! What shall we do then? Eh?

SWINDON [*sullenly*] Our duty, sir, I presume.

BURGOYNE [*again sarcastic—giving him up as a fool*] Quite so, quite so. Thank you, Major Swindon, thank you. Now youve settled the question, sir—thrown a flood of light on the situation. What a comfort to me to feel that I have at my side so devoted and able an officer to support me in this emergency! I think, sir, it will probably relieve both our feelings if we proceed to hang this dissenter without further delay [*he strikes the bell*] especially as I am debarred by my principles from the customary military vent for my feelings. [*The sergeant appears*]. Bring your man in.

SERGEANT. Yes, sir.

BURGOYNE. And mention to any officer you may meet that the court cannot wait any longer for him.

SWINDQN [*keeping his temper with difficulty*] The staff is perfectly ready, sir. They have been waiting your convenience for fully half an hour. Perfectly ready, sir.

BURGOYNE [*blandly*] So am I. [*Several officers come in and take their seats. One of them sits at the end of the table farthest from the door, and acts throughout as clerk of the court, making notes of the proceedings. The uniforms are those of the 9th, 20th, 21st, 24th, 47th, 53rd, and 62nd British Infantry. One officer is a Major General of the Royal Artillery. There are also German officers of the Hessian Rifles, and of German dragoon and Brunswicker regiments*]. Oh, good morning, gentlemen. Sorry to disturb you, I am sure. Very good of you to spare us a few moments.

SWINDON. Will you preside, sir?

BURGOYNE [*becoming additionally polished, lofty, sarcastic, and urbane now that he is in public*] No, sir: I feel my own deficiencies too keenly to presume so far. If you will kindly allow me, I will sit at the feet of Gamaliel. [*He takes the chair at the end of the table next the door, and motions Swindon to the chair of state, waiting for him to be seated before sitting down himself*].

SWINDON [*greatly annoyed*] As you please, sir. I am only trying to do my duty under excessively trying circumstances. [*He takes his place in the chair of state*].

Burgoyne, relaxing his studied demeanor for the moment, sits down and begins to read the report with knitted brows and careworn looks, reflecting on his desperate situation and Swindon's uselessness. Richard is brought in. Judith walks beside him. Two soldiers precede and two follow him, with the sergeant in command. They cross the room to the wall opposite the door; but when Richard has just passed before the chair of state the sergeant stops him with a touch on the arm, and posts himself behind him, at his elbow. Judith stands timidly at the wall. The four soldiers place themselves in a squad near her.

BURGOYNE [*looking up and seeing Judith*] Who is that woman?

SERGEANT. Prisoner's wife, sir.

SWINDON [*nervously*] She begged me to allow her to be present; and I thought—

BURGOYNE [*completing the sentence for him ironically*] You thought it would be a pleasure for her. Quite so, quite so. [*Blandly*] Give the lady a chair; and make her thoroughly comfortable.

The sergeant fetches a chair and places it near Richard.

JUDITH. Thank you, sir. [*She sits down after an awestricken curtsy to Burgoyne, which he acknowledges by a dignified bend of his head*].

SWINDON [*to Richard, sharply*] Your name, sir?

RICHARD [*affable, but obstinate*] Come: you dont mean to say that youve brought me here without knowing who I am?

SWINDON. As a matter of form, sir, give your name.

RICHARD. As a matter of form then, my name is Anthony Anderson, Presbyterian minister in this town.

BURGOYNE [*interested*] Indeed! Pray, Mr Anderson, what do you gentlemen believe?

RICHARD. I shall be happy to explain if time is allowed me. I cannot undertake to complete your conversion in less than a fortnight.

SWINDON [*snubbing him*] We are not here to discuss your views.

BURGOYNE [*with an elaborate bow to the unfortunate Swindon*] I stand rebuked.

SWINDON [*embarrassed*] Oh, not you, I as—

BURGOYNE. Dont mention it. [*To Richard, very politely*] Any political views, Mr Anderson?

RICHARD. I understand that that is just what we are here to find out.

SWINDON [*severely*] Do you mean to deny that you are a rebel?

RICHARD. I am an American, sir.

SWINDON. What do you expect me to think of that speech, Mr Anderson?

RICHARD. I never expect a soldier to think, sir.

77

Burgoyne is boundlessly delighted by this retort, which almost reconciles him to the loss of America.

SWINDON [*whitening with anger*] I advise you not to be insolent, prisoner.

RICHARD. You cant help yourself, General. When you make up your mind to hang a man, you put yourself at a disadvantage with him. Why should I be civil to you? I may as well be hanged for a sheep as a lamb.

SWINDON. You have no right to assume that the court has made up its mind without a fair trial. And you will please not address me as General. I am Major Swindon.

RICHARD. A thousand pardons. I thought I had the honor of addressing Gentlemanly Johnny.

Sensation among the officers. The sergeant has a narrow escape from a guffaw.

BURGOYNE [*with extreme suavity*] I believe I am Gentlemanly Johnny, sir, at your service. My more intimate friends call me General Burgoyne. [*Richard bows with perfect politeness*]. You will understand, sir, I hope, since you seem to be a gentleman and a man of some spirit in spite of your calling, that if we should have the misfortune to hang you, we shall do so as a mere matter of political necessity and military duty, without any personal ill-feeling.

RICHARD. Oh, quite so. That makes all the difference in the world, of course.

They all smile in spite of themselves; and some of the younger officers burst out laughing.

JUDITH [*her dread and horror deepening at every one of these jests and compliments*] How can you?

RICHARD. You promised to be silent.

BURGOYNE [*to Judith, with studied courtesy*] Believe me, Madam, your husband is placing us under the greatest obligation by taking this very disagreeable business so thoroughly in the spirit of a gentleman. Sergeant: give Mr Anderson a chair. [*The sergeant does so. Richard sits down*]. Now, Major Swindon: we are waiting for you.

THE DEVIL'S DISCIPLE

SWINDON. You are aware, I presume, Mr Anderson, of your obligations as a subject of His Majesty King George the Third.

RICHARD. I am aware, sir, that His Majesty King George the Third is about to hang me because I object to Lord North's robbing me.

SWINDON. That is a treasonable speech, sir.

RICHARD [*briefly*] Yes. I meant it to be.

BURGOYNE [*strongly deprecating this line of defence, but still polite*] Dont you think, Mr Anderson, that this is rather—if you will excuse the word—a vulgar line to take? Why should you cry out robbery because of a stamp duty and a tea duty and so forth? After all, it is the essence of your position as a gentleman that you pay with a good grace.

RICHARD. It is not the money, General. But to be swindled by a pig-headed lunatic like King George—

SWINDON [*scandalized*] Chut, sir—silence!

SERGEANT [*in stentorian tones, greatly shocked*] Silence!

BURGOYNE [*unruffled*] Ah, this is another point of view. My position does not allow of my going into that, except in private. But [*shrugging his shoulders*] of course, Mr Anderson, if you are determined to be hanged [*Judith flinches*] there's nothing more to be said. An unusual taste! however [*with a final shrug*]—!

SWINDON [*To Burgoyne*] Shall we call witnesses?

RICHARD. What need is there of witnesses? If the townspeople here had listened to me, you would have found the streets barricaded, the houses loopholed, and the people in arms to hold the town against you to the last man. But you arrived, unfortunately, before we had got out of the talking stage; and then it was too late.

SWINDON [*severely*] Well, sir, we shall teach you and your townspeople a lesson they will not forget. Have you anything more to say?

RICHARD. I think you might have the decency to treat me as a prisoner of war, and shoot me like a man instead of hanging me like a dog.

BURGOYNE [*sympathetically*] Now there, Mr Anderson, you

talk like a civilian, if you will excuse my saying so. Have you any idea of the average marksmanship of the army of His Majesty King George the Third? If we make you up a firing party, what will happen? Half of them will miss you: the rest will make a mess of the business and leave you to the provo-marshal's pistol. Whereas we can hang you in a perfectly workmanlike and agreeable way. [*Kindly*] Let me persuade you to be hanged, Mr Anderson?

JUDITH [*sick with horror*] My God!

RICHARD [*To Judith*] Your promise! [*To Burgoyne*] Thank you, General: that view of the case did not occur to me before. To oblige you, I withdraw my objection to the rope. Hang me, by all means.

BURGOYNE [*smoothly*] Will 12 o'clock suit you, Mr Anderson?

RICHARD. I shall be at your disposal then, General.

BURGOYNE [*rising*] Nothing more to be said, gentlemen. [*They all rise*].

JUDITH [*rushing to the table*] Oh, you are not going to murder a man like that, without a proper trial—without thinking of what you are doing—without—[*she cannot find words*].

RICHARD. Is this how you keep your promise?

JUDITH. If I am not to speak, you must. Defend yourself: save yourself: tell them the truth.

RICHARD [*worriedly*] I have told them truth enough to hang me ten times over. If you say another word you will risk other lives; but you will not save mine.

BURGOYNE. My good lady, our only desire is to save unpleasantness. What satisfaction would it give you to have a solemn fuss made, with my friend Swindon in a black cap and so forth? I am sure we are greatly indebted to the admirable tact and gentlemanly feeling shewn by your husband.

JUDITH [*throwing the words in his face*] Oh, you are mad. Is it nothing to you what wicked thing you do if only you do it like a gentleman? Is it nothing to you whether you are a murderer or not, if only you murder in a red coat? [*Desperately*] You shall not hang him: that man is not my husband.

The officers look at one another, and whisper: some of the Germans asking their neighbors to explain what the woman had said. Burgoyne, who has been visibly shaken by Judith's reproach, recovers himself promptly at this new development. Richard meanwhile raises his voice above the buzz.

RICHARD. I appeal to you, gentlemen, to put an end to this. She will not believe that she cannot save me. Break up the court.

BURGOYNE [*in a voice so quiet and firm that it restores silence at once*] One moment, Mr Anderson. One moment, gentlemen. [*He resumes his seat. Swindon and the officers follow his example*]. Let me understand you clearly, madam. Do you mean that this gentleman is not your husband, or merely—I wish to put this with all delicacy—that you are not his wife?

JUDITH. I dont know what you mean. I say that he is not my husband—that my husband has escaped. This man took his place to save him. Ask anyone in the town—send out into the street for the first person you find there, and bring him in as a witness. He will tell you that the prisoner is not Anthony Anderson.

BURGOYNE [*quietly, as before*] Sergeant.

SERGEANT. Yes, sir.

BURGOYNE. Go out into the street and bring in the first townsman you see there.

SERGEANT [*making for the door*] Yes, sir.

BURGOYNE [*as the sergeant passes*] The first clean, sober townsman you see.

SERGEANT. Yes, sir. [*He goes out*].

BURGOYNE. Sit down, Mr Anderson—if I may call you so for the present. [*Richard sits down*]. Sit down, madam, whilst we wait. Give the lady a newspaper.

RICHARD [*indignantly*] Shame!

BURGOYNE [*keenly, with a half smile*] If you are not her husband, sir, the case is not a serious one—for her [*Richard bites his lip, silenced*].

JUDITH [*to Richard, as she returns to her seat*] I couldnt help it. [*He shakes his head. She sits down*].

BURGOYNE. You will understand of course, Mr Anderson, that you must not build on this little incident. We are bound to make an example of somebody.

RICHARD. I quite understand. I suppose theres no use in my explaining.

BURGOYNE. I think we should prefer independent testimony, if you dont mind.

The sergeant, with a packet of papers in his hand, returns conducting Christy, who is much scared.

SERGEANT [*giving Burgoyne the packet*] Dispatches, sir. Delivered by a corporal of the 33rd. Dead beat with hard riding, sir.

Burgoyne opens the dispatches, and presently becomes absorbed in them. They are so serious as to take his attention completely from the court martial.

THE SERGEANT [*to Christy*] Now then. Attention; and take your hat off. [*He posts himself in charge of Christy, who stands on Burgoyne's side of the court*].

RICHARD [*in his usual bullying tone to Christy*] Dont be frightened, you fool: youre only wanted as a witness. Theyre not going to hang you.

SWINDON. Whats your name?

CHRISTY. Christy.

RICHARD [*impatiently*] Christopher Dudgeon, you blatant idiot. Give your full name.

SWINDON. Be silent, prisoner. You must not prompt the witness.

RICHARD. Very well. But I warn you youll get nothing out of him unless you shake it out of him. He has been too well brought up by a pious mother to have any sense or manhood left in him.

BURGOYNE [*springing up and speaking to the sergeant in a startling voice*] Where is the man who brought these?

SERGEANT. In the guard-room, sir.

Burgoyne goes out with a haste that sets the officers exchanging looks.

SWINDON [*to Christy*] Do you know Anthony Anderson, the Presbyterian minister?

CHRISTY. Of course I do [*implying that Swindon must be an ass not to know it*].

SWINDON. Is he here?

CHRISTY [*staring round*] I dont know.

SWINDON. Do you see him?

CHRISTY. No.

SWINDON. You seem to know the prisoner?

CHRISTY. Do you mean Dick?

SWINDON. Which is Dick?

CHRISTY [*pointing to Richard*] Him.

SWINDON. What is his name?

CHRISTY. Dick.

RICHARD. Answer properly, you jumping jackass. What do they know about Dick?

CHRISTY. Well, you are Dick, aint you? What am I to say?

SWINDON. Address me, sir; and do you, prisoner, be silent. Tell us who the prisoner is.

CHRISTY. He's my brother Dick—Richard—Richard Dudgeon.

SWINDON. Your brother!

CHRISTY. Yes.

SWINDON. You are sure he is not Anderson.

CHRISTY. Who?

RICHARD [*exasperatedly*] Me, me, me, you—

SWINDON. Silence, sir.

SERGEANT [*shouting*] Silence.

RICHARD [*impatiently*] Yah! [*To Christy*] He wants to know am I Minister Anderson. Tell him, and stop grinning like a zany.

CHRISTY [*grinning more than ever*] You Pastor Anderson! [*To Swindon*] Why, Mr Anderson's a minister—a very good man; and Dick's a bad character: the respectable people wont speak to him. He's the bad brother: I'm the good one. [*The officers laugh outright. The soldiers grin*].

SWINDON. Who arrested this man?

SERGEANT. I did, sir. I found him in the minister's house, sitting at tea with the lady with his coat off, quite at home. If he isnt married to her, he ought to be.

SWINDON. Did he answer to the minister's name?

SERGEANT. Yes, sir, but not to a minister's nature. You ask the chaplain, sir.

SWINDON [to Richard, threateningly] So, sir, you have attempted to cheat us. And your name is Richard Dudgeon?

RICHARD. Youve found it out at last, have you?

SWINDON. Dudgeon is a name well known to us, eh?

RICHARD. Yes: Peter Dudgeon, whom you murdered, was my uncle.

SWINDON. Hm! [He compresses his lips, and looks at Richard with vindictive gravity].

CHRISTY. Are they going to hang you, Dick?

RICHARD. Yes. Get out: theyve done with you.

CHRISTY. And I may keep the china peacocks?

RICHARD [jumping up] Get out. Get out, you blithering baboon, you. [Christy flies, panicstricken].

SWINDON [rising—all rise] Since you have taken the minister's place, Richard Dudgeon, you shall go through with it. The execution will take place at 12 o'clock as arranged; and unless Anderson surrenders before then, you shall take his place on the gallows. Sergeant: take your man out.

JUDITH [distracted] No, no—

SWINDON [fiercely, dreading a renewal of her entreaties] Take that woman away.

RICHARD [springing across the table with a tiger-like bound, and seizing Swindon by the throat] You infernal scoundrel—

The sergeant rushes to the rescue from one side, the soldiers from the other. They seize Richard and drag him back to his place. Swindon, who has been thrown supine on the table, rises, arranging his stock. He is about to speak, when he is anticipated by Burgoyne, who has just appeared at the door with two papers in his hand: a white letter and a blue dispatch.

BURGOYNE [*advancing to the table, elaborately cool*] What is this? Whats happening? Mr Anderson: I'm astonished at you.

RICHARD. I am sorry I disturbed you, General. I merely wanted to strangle your understrapper there. [*Breaking out violently at Swindon*] Why do you raise the devil in me by bullying the woman like that? You oatmeal faced dog, I'd twist your cursed head off with the greatest satisfaction. [*He puts out his hands to the sergeant*] Here: handcuff me, will you; or I'll not undertake to keep my fingers off him.

The sergeant takes out a pair of handcuffs and looks to Burgoyne for instructions.

BURGOYNE. Have you addressed profane language to the lady, Major Swindon?

SWINDON [*very angry*] No, sir, certainly not. That question should not have been put to me. I ordered the woman to be removed, as she was disorderly; and the fellow sprang at me. Put away those handcuffs. I am perfectly able to take care of myself.

RICHARD. Now you talk like a man, I have no quarrel with you.

BURGOYNE. Mr Anderson—

SWINDON. His name is Dudgeon, sir, Richard Dudgeon. He is an impostor.

BURGOYNE [*brusquely*] Nonsense, sir: you hanged Dudgeon at Springtown.

RICHARD. It was my uncle, General.

BURGOYNE. Oh, your uncle. [*To Swindon, handsomely*] I beg your pardon, Major Swindon. [*Swindon acknowledges the apology stiffly. Burgoyne turns to Richard*]. We are somewhat unfortunate in our relations with your family. Well, Mr Dudgeon, what I wanted to ask you is this. Who is [*reading the name from the letter*] William Maindeck Parshotter?

RICHARD. He is the Mayor of Springtown.

BURGOYNE. Is William—Maindeck and so on—a man of his word?

RICHARD. Is he selling you anything?

BURGOYNE. No.

RICHARD. Then you may depend on him.

BURGOYNE. Thank you, Mr—'m Dudgeon. By the way, since you are not Mr Anderson, do we still—eh, Major Swindon? [*meaning "do we still hang him?"*]

RICHARD. The arrangements are unaltered, General.

BURGOYNE. Ah, indeed. I am sorry. Good morning, Mr Dudgeon. Good morning, madam.

RICHARD [*interrupting Judith almost fiercely as she is about to make some wild appeal, and taking her arm resolutely*] Not one word more. Come.

She looks imploringly at him, but is overborne by his determination. They are marched out by the four soldiers: the sergeant very sulky, walking between Swindon and Richard, whom he watches as if he were a dangerous animal.

BURGOYNE. Gentlemen: we need not detain you. Major Swindon: a word with you. [*The officers go out. Burgoyne waits with unruffled serenity until the last of them disappears. Then he becomes very grave, and addresses Swindon for the first time without his title*]. Swindon: do you know what this is [*shewing him the letter*]?

SWINDON. What?

BURGOYNE. A demand for a safe-conduct for an officer of their militia to come here and arrange terms with us.

SWINDON. Oh, they are giving in.

BURGOYNE. They add that they are sending the man who raised Springtown last night and drove us out; so that we may know that we are dealing with an officer of importance.

SWINDON. Pooh!

BURGOYNE. He will be fully empowered to arrange the terms of —guess what.

SWINDON. Their surrender, I hope.

BURGOYNE. No: our evacuation of the town. They offer us just six hours to clear out.

SWINDON. What monstrous impudence!

BURGOYNE. What shall we do, eh?

THE DEVIL'S DISCIPLE

SWINDON. March on Springtown and strike a decisive blow at once.

BURGOYNE [*quietly*] Hm! [*Turning to the door*] Come to the adjutant's office.

SWINDON. What for?

BURGOYNE. To write out that safe-conduct. [*He puts his hand to the door knob to open it*].

SWINDON [*who has not budged*] General Burgoyne.

BURGOYNE [*returning*] Sir?

SWINDON. It is my duty to tell you, sir, that I do not consider the threats of a mob of rebellious tradesmen a sufficient reason for our giving way.

BURGOYNE [*imperturbable*] Suppose I resign my command to you, what will you do?

SWINDON. I will undertake to do what we have marched south from Quebec to do, and what General Howe has marched north from New York to do: effect a junction at Albany and wipe out the rebel army with our united forces.

BURGOYNE [*enigmatically*] And will you wipe out our enemies in London, too?

SWINDON. In London! What enemies?

BURGOYNE [*forcibly*] Jobbery and snobbery, incompetence and Red Tape. [*He holds up the dispatch and adds, with despair in his face and voice*] I have just learnt, sir, that General Howe is still in New York.

SWINDON [*thunderstruck*] Good God! He has disobeyed orders!

BURGOYNE [*with sardonic calm*] He has received no orders, sir. Some gentleman in London forgot to dispatch them: he was leaving town for his holiday, I believe. To avoid upsetting his arrangements, England will lose her American colonies; and in a few days you and I will be at Saratoga with 5,000 men to face 18,000 rebels in an impregnable position.

SWINDON [*appalled*] Impossible?

BURGOYNE [*coldly*] I beg your pardon?

SWINDON. I cant believe it! What will History say?

BURGOYNE. History, sir, will tell lies, as usual. Come: we must send the safe-conduct. [*He goes out*].

SWINDON [*following distractedly*] My God, my God! We shall be wiped out.

As noon approaches there is excitement in the market place. The gallows which hang there permanently for the terror of evildoers, with such minor advertizers and examples of crime as the pillory, the whipping post, and the stocks, has a new rope attached, with the noose hitched up to one of the uprights, out of reach of the boys. Its ladder, too, has been brought out and placed in position by the town beadle, who stands by to guard it from unauthorized climbing. The Webster-bridge townsfolk are present in force, and in high spirits; for the news has spread that it is the devil's disciple and not the minister that King George and his terrible general are about to hang: consequently the execution can be enjoyed without any misgiving as to its righteousness, or to the cowardice of allowing it to take place without a struggle. There is even some fear of a disappointment as midday approaches and the arrival of the beadle with the ladder remains the only sign of preparation. But at last reassuring shouts of Here they come: Here they are, are heard; and a company of soldiers with fixed bayonets, half British infantry, half Hessians, tramp quickly into the middle of the market place, driving the crowd to the sides.

THE SERGEANT. Halt, Front. Dress. [*The soldiers change their column into a square enclosing the gallows, their petty officers, energetically led by the sergeant, hustling the persons who find themselves inside the square out at the corners*]. Now then! Out of it with you: out of it. Some o youll get strung up yourselves presently. Form that square there, will you, you damned Hoosians. No use talkin German to them: talk to their toes with the butt ends of your muskets: theyll understand that. Get out of it, will you. [*He comes upon Judith, standing near the gallows*]. Now then: youve no call here.

JUDITH. May I not stay? What harm am I doing?

SERGEANT. I want none of your argufying. You ought to be ashamed of yourself, running to see a man hanged thats not your husband. And he's no better than yourself. I told my major he was a gentleman; and then he goes and tries to strangle him, and calls his blessed Majesty a lunatic. So out of it with you, double quick.

JUDITH. Will you take these two silver dollars and let me stay?

The sergeant, without an instant's hesitation, looks quickly and furtively round as he shoots the money dexterously into his pocket. Then he raises his voice in virtuous indignation.

THE SERGEANT. Me take money in the execution of my duty! Certainly not. Now I'll tell you what I'll do, to teach you to corrupt the King's officer. I'll put you under arrest until the execution's over. You just stand there; and dont let me see you as much as move from that spot until youre let. [*With a swift wink at her he points to the corner of the square behind the gallows on his right, and turns noisily away, shouting*] Now then, dress up and keep em back, will you.

Cries of Hush and Silence are heard among the townsfolk; and the sound of a military band, playing the Dead March from Saul, is heard. The crowd becomes quiet at once; and the sergeant and petty officers, hurrying to the back of the square, with a few whispered orders and some stealthy hustling cause it to open and admit the funeral procession, which is protected from the crowd by a double file of soldiers. First come Burgoyne and Swindon, who, on entering the square, glance with distaste at the gallows, and avoid passing under it by wheeling a little to the right and stationing themselves on that side. Then Mr Brudenell, the chaplain, in his surplice, with his prayer book open in his hand, walking beside Richard, who is moody and disorderly. He walks doggedly through the gallows framework, and posts himself a little in front of it. Behind him comes the executioner, a stalwart soldier in his shirtsleeves. Following him, two soldiers haul a light military waggon. Finally comes the band, which posts itself at the back of the square, and finishes the Dead March. Judith, watching Richard, painfully steals down to the gallows, and stands leaning against its right post. During the conversation which follows, the two soldiers place the cart under the gallows, and stand by the shafts, which point backwards. The executioner takes a set of steps from the cart and places it ready for the prisoner to mount. Then he climbs the tall ladder which stands against the gallows, and cuts the string by which the rope is hitched up; so that the noose drops dangling over the cart, into which he steps as he descends.

RICHARD [*with suppressed impatience to Brudenell*] Look here, sir: this is no place for a man of your profession. Hadnt you better go away?

SWINDON. I appeal to you, prisoner, if you have any sense of decency left, to listen to the ministrations of the chaplain, and pay due heed to the solemnity of the occasion.

THE CHAPLAIN [*gently reproving Richard*] Try to control yourself, and submit to the divine will. [*He lifts his book to proceed with the service*].

RICHARD. Answer for your own will, sir, and those of your accomplices here [*indicating Burgoyne and Swindon*]: I see little divinity about them or you. You talk to me of Christianity when you are in the act of hanging your enemies. Was there ever such blasphemous nonsense! [*To Swindon, more rudely*] Youve got up the solemnity of the occasion, as you call it, to impress the people with your own dignity—Handel's music and a clergyman to make murder look like piety! Do you suppose *I* am going to help you? Youve asked me to choose the rope because you dont know your own trade well enough to shoot me properly. Well, hang away and have done with it.

SWINDON [*to the chaplain*] Can you do nothing with him, Mr Brudenell?

CHAPLAIN. I will try, sir. [*Beginning to read*] Man that is born of woman hath—

RICHARD [*fixing his eyes on him*] "Thou shalt not kill."

The book drops in Brudenell's hands.

CHAPLAIN [*confessing his embarrassment*] What am I to say, Mr Dudgeon?

RICHARD. Let me alone, cant you?

BURGOYNE [*with extreme urbanity*] I think, Mr Brudenell, that as the usual professional observations seem to strike Mr Dudgeon as incongruous under the circumstances, you had better omit them until—er—until Mr Dudgeon can no longer be inconvenienced by them. [*Brudenell, with a shrug, shuts his book and retires behind the gallows*]. You seem in a hurry, Mr Dudgeon.

RICHARD [*with the horror of death upon him*] Do you think this is a pleasant sort of thing to be kept waiting for? Youve made up your mind to commit murder: well, do it and have done with it.

BURGOYNE. Mr Dudgeon: we are only doing this—

RICHARD. Because youre paid to do it.

SWINDON. You insolent— [*he swallows his rage*].

BURGOYNE [*with much charm of manner*] Ah, I am really sorry that you should think that, Mr Dudgeon. If you knew what my commission cost me, and what my pay is, you would think better of me. I should be glad to part from you on friendly terms.

RICHARD. Hark ye, General Burgoyne. If you think that I like being hanged, youre mistaken. I dont like it; and I dont mean to pretend that I do. And if you think I'm obliged to you for hanging me in a gentlemanly way, youre wrong there too. I take the whole business in devilish bad part; and the only satisfaction I have in it is that youll feel a good deal meaner than I'll look when it's over. [*He turns away, and is striding to the cart when Judith advances and interposes with her arms stretched out to him. Richard, feeling that a very little will upset his self-possession, shrinks from her, crying*] What are you doing here? This is no place for you. [*She makes a gesture as if to touch him. He recoils impatiently*] No: go away, go away: youll unnerve me. Take her away, will you.

JUDITH. Wont you bid me goodbye?

RICHARD [*allowing her to take his hand*] Oh goodbye, goodbye. Now go—go—quickly. [*She clings to his hand—will not be put off with so cold a last farewell—at last, as he tries to disengage himself, throws herself on his breast in agony*].

SWINDON [*angrily to the sergeant, who, alarmed at Judith's movement, has come from the back of the square to pull her back, and stopped irresolutely on finding that he is too late*] How is this? Why is she inside the lines?

SERGEANT [*guiltily*] I dunno, sir. She's that artful—cant keep her away.

BURGOYNE. You were bribed.

SERGEANT [*protesting*] No, sir—

SWINDON [*severely*] Fall back. [*He obeys*].

RICHARD [*imploringly to those around him, and finally to Burgoyne, as the least stolid of them*] Take her away. Do you think I want a woman near me now?

BURGOYNE [*going to Judith and taking her hand*] Here, madam: you had better keep inside the lines; but stand here behind us; and dont look.

Richard, with a great sobbing sigh of relief as she releases him and turns to Burgoyne, flies for refuge to the cart and mounts into it. The executioner takes off his coat and pinions him.

JUDITH [*resisting Burgoyne quietly and drawing her hand away*] No: I must stay. I wont look. [*She goes to the right of the gallows. She tries to look at Richard, but turns away with a frightful shudder, and falls on her knees in prayer. Brudenell comes towards her from the back of the square*].

BURGOYNE [*nodding approvingly as she kneels*] Ah, quite so. Do not disturb her, Mr Brudenell: that will do very nicely. [*Brudenell nods also, and withdraws a little, watching her sympathetically. Burgoyne resumes his former position, and takes out a handsome gold chronometer*]. Now then, are those preparations made? We must not detain Mr Dudgeon.

By this time Richard's hands are bound behind him; and the noose is round his neck. The two soldiers take the shafts of the waggon, ready to pull it away. The executioner, standing in the cart behind Richard, makes a sign to the sergeant.

SERGEANT [*to Burgoyne*] Ready, sir.

BURGOYNE. Have you anything more to say, Mr Dudgeon? It wants two minutes of twelve still.

RICHARD [*in a strong voice of a man who has conquered the bitterness of death*] Your watch is two minutes slow by the town clock, which I can see from here, General. [*The town clock strikes the first stroke of twelve. Involuntarily the people flinch at the sound, and a subdued groan breaks from them*]. Amen! my life for the world's future!

ANDERSON [*shouting as he rushes into the market place*] Amen; and stop the execution. [*He bursts through the line of soldiers opposite Burgoyne, and rushes, panting, to the gallows*]. I am Anthony Anderson, the man you want.

The crowd, intensely excited, listens with all its ears. Judith, half rising, stares at him; then lifts her hands like one whose dearest prayer has been granted.

SWINDON. Indeed. Then you are just in time to take your place on the gallows. Arrest him.

At a sign from the sergeant, two soldiers come forward to seize Anderson.

ANDERSON [*thrusting a paper under Swindon's nose*] Theres my safe-conduct, sir.

SWINDON [*taken aback*] Safe-conduct! Are you—!

ANDERSON [*emphatically*] I am. [*The two soldiers take him by the elbows*]. Tell these men to take their hands off me.

SWINDON [*to the men*] Let him go.

SERGEANT. Fall back.

The two men return to their places. The townsfolk raise a cheer; and begin to exchange exultant looks, with a presentiment of triumph as they see their Pastor speaking with their enemies in the gate.

ANDERSON [*exhaling a deep breath of relief, and dabbing his perspiring brow with his handkerchief*] Thank God, I was in time!

BURGOYNE [*calm as ever, and still watch in hand*] Ample time, sir. Plenty of time. I should never dream of hanging any gentleman by an American clock. [*He puts up his watch*].

ANDERSON. Yes: we are some minutes ahead of you already, General. Now tell them to take the rope from the neck of that American citizen.

BURGOYNE [*to the executioner in the cart—very politely*] Kindly undo Mr Dudgeon.

The executioner takes the rope from Richard's neck, unties his hands, and helps him on with his coat.

JUDITH [*stealing timidly to Anderson*] Tony.

ANDERSON [*putting his arm round her shoulders and bantering her affectionately*] Well, what do you think of your husband n o w, eh?—eh??—eh???

JUDITH. I am ashamed—[*she hides her face against his breast*].

BURGOYNE [*to Swindon*] You look disappointed, Major Swindon.

SWINDON. You look defeated, General Burgoyne.

BURGOYNE. I am, sir; and I am humane enough to be glad of it. [*Richard jumps down from the cart, Brudenell offering his hand to help him, and runs to Anderson, whose left hand he shakes heartily, the right being occupied by Judith*]. By the way, Mr Anderson, I do not quite understand. The safe-conduct was for a commander of the militia. I understand you are a—[*He looks as pointedly as his good manners permit at the riding boots, the pistols, and Richard's coat, and adds*]—a clergyman.

ANDERSON [*between Judith and Richard*] Sir; it is in the hour of trial that a man finds his true profession. This foolish young man [*placing his hand on Richard's shoulder*] boasted himself the Devil's Disciple; but when the hour of trial came to him, he found that it was his destiny to suffer and be faithful to the death. I thought myself a decent minister of the gospel of peace; but when the hour of trial came to me, I found that it was my destiny to be a man of action, and that my place was amid the thunder of the captains and the shouting. So I am starting life at fifty as Captain Anthony Anderson of the Springtown militia; and the Devil's Disciple here will start presently as the Reverend Richard Dudgeon, and wag his pow in my old pulpit, and give good advice to this silly sentimental little wife of mine [*putting his other hand on her shoulder. She steals a glance at Richard to see how the prospect pleases him*]. Your mother told me, Richard, that I should never have chosen Judith if I'd been born for the ministry. I am afraid she was right; so, by your leave, you may keep my coat and I'll keep yours.

RICHARD. Minister—I should say Captain. I have behaved like a fool.

JUDITH. Like a hero.

RICHARD. Much the same thing, perhaps. [*With some bitterness towards himself*] But no: if I had been any good, I should have done for you what you did for me, instead of making a vain sacrifice.

ANDERSON. Not vain, my boy. It takes all sorts to make a world —saints as well as soldiers. [*Turning to Burgoyne*] And now, General, time presses; and America is in a hurry. Have you realized that though you may occupy towns and win battles, you cannot conquer a nation?

BURGOYNE. My good sir, without a Conquest you cannot have an aristocracy. Come and settle the matter at my quarters.

ANDERSON. At your service, sir. [*To Richard*] See Judith home for me, will you, my boy. [*He hands her over to him*]. Now, General. [*He goes busily up the market place towards the Town Hall, leaving Judith and Richard together. Burgoyne follows him a step or two; then checks himself and turns to Richard*].

BURGOYNE. Oh, by the way, Mr Dudgeon, I shall be glad to see you at lunch at half-past one. [*He pauses a moment and adds, with politely veiled slyness*] Bring Mrs Anderson, if she will be so good. [*To Swindon, who is fuming*] Take it quietly, Major Swindon: your friend the British soldier can stand up to anything except the British War Office. [*He follows Anderson*].

SERGEANT [*to Swindon*] What orders, sir?

SWINDON [*savagely*] Orders! What use are orders now! Theres no army. Back to quarters; and be d— [*He turns on his heel and goes*].

SERGEANT [*pugnacious and patriotic, repudiating the idea of defeat*] 'Tention. Now then: cock up your chins, and shew em you dont care a damn for em. Slope arms! Fours! Wheel! Quick march!

The drums mark time with a tremendous bang; the band strikes up British Grenadiers; and the Sergeant, Brudenell, and the English

THE DEVIL'S DISCIPLE

troops march off defiantly to their quarters. The townsfolk press in behind, and follow them up the market, jeering at them; and the town band, a very primitive affair, brings up the rear, playing Yankee Doodle. Essie, who comes in with them, runs to Richard.

ESSIE. Oh, Dick!

RICHARD [*good-humoredly, but wilfully*] Now, now: come, come! I dont mind being hanged: but I will not be cried over.

ESSIE. No, I promise. I'll be good. [*She tries to restrain her tears, but cannot*]. I—I want to see where the soldiers are going to. [*She goes a little way up the market, pretending to look after the crowd*].

JUDITH. Promise me you will never tell him.

RICHARD. Dont be afraid.

They shake hands on it.

ESSIE [*calling to them*] Theyre coming back. They want you.

Jubilation in the market. The townsfolk surge back again in wild enthusiasm with their band, and hoist Richard on their shoulders, cheering him.

SHAW'S NOTES TO THE DEVIL'S DISCIPLE
BURGOYNE

GENERAL JOHN BURGOYNE, who is presented in this play for the first time (as far as I am aware) on the English stage, is not a conventional stage soldier, but as faithful a portrait as it is in the nature of stage portraits to be. His objection to profane swearing is not borrowed from Mr Gilbert's H.M.S. Pinafore: it is taken from the Code of Instructions drawn up by himself for his officers when he introduced Light Horse into the English Army. His opinion that English soldiers should be treated as thinking beings was no doubt as unwelcome to the military authorities of his time, when nothing was thought of ordering a soldier a thousand lashes, as it will be to those modern victims of the flagellation neurosis who are so anxious to revive that discredited sport. His military reports are very clever as criticisms, and are humane and enlightened within certain aristocratic limits, best illustrated perhaps by his declaration, which now sounds so curious, that he should blush to ask for promotion on any other ground than that of family influence. As a parliamentary candidate, Burgoyne took our common expression "fighting an election" so very literally that he led his supporters to the poll at Preston in 1768 with a loaded pistol in each hand, and won the seat, though he was fined £1000, and denounced by Junius, for the pistols.

It is only within quite recent years that any general recognition has become possible for the feeling that led Burgoyne, a professed enemy of oppression in India and elsewhere, to accept his American command when so many other officers threw up their commissions rather than serve in a civil war against the Colonies. His biographer De Fonblanque, writing in 1876, evidently regarded his position as indefensible. Nowadays, it is sufficient to say that Burgoyne was an Imperialist. He sympathized with the colonists; but when they proposed as a remedy the disruption of the Empire, he regarded that as a step backward in civilization. As he put it to

97

the House of Commons, "while we remember that we are contending against brothers and fellow subjects, we must also remember that we are contending in this crisis for the fate of the British Empire." Eightyfour years after his defeat, his republican conquerors themselves engaged in a civil war for the integrity of their Union. In 1885 the Whigs who represented the anti-Burgoyne tradition of American Independence in English politics, abandoned Gladstone and made common cause with their political opponents in defence of the Union between England and Ireland. Only the other day England sent 200,000 men into the field south of the equator to fight out the question whether South Africa should develop as a Federation of British Colonies or as an independent Afrikander United States. In all these cases the Unionists who were detached from their parties were called renegades, as Burgoyne was. That, of course, is only one of the unfortunate consequences of the fact that mankind, being for the most part incapable of politics, accepts vituperation as an easy and congenial substitute. Whether Burgoyne or Washington, Lincoln or Davis, Gladstone or Bright, Mr Chamberlain or Mr Leonard Courtney was in the right will never be settled, because it will never be possible to prove that the government of the victor has been better for mankind than the government of the vanquished would have been. It is true that the victors have no doubt on the point; but to the dramatist, that certainty of theirs is only part of the human comedy. The American Unionist is often a Separatist as to Ireland; the English Unionist often sympathizes with the Polish Home Ruler; and both English and American Unionists are apt to be Disruptionists as regards that Imperial Ancient of Days, the Empire of China. Both are Unionists concerning Canada, but with a difference as to the precise application to it of the Monroe doctrine. As for me, the dramatist, I smile, and lead the conversation back to Burgoyne.

Burgoyne's surrender at Saratoga made him that occasionally necessary part of our British system, a scapegoat. The explanation of his defeat given in the play (p. 87) is founded on a passage quoted by De Fonblanque from Fitzmaurice's Life of Lord Shelburne, as follows: "Lord George Germain, having among other peculiarities a particular dislike to be put out of his way on any occasion, had arranged to call at his office on his way to the country to sign the dispatches; but as those addressed to Howe had not been fair-copied, and he was not disposed to be balked of his projected visit to Kent, they were not signed then and were forgotten on his return home." These were the dispatches instructing Sir William Howe, who was in New York, to effect a junction at Albany with Burgoyne, who had marched from Quebec for that purpose. Burgoyne got as far as Saratoga, where, failing the expected reinforcement, he was hopelessly outnumbered, and his officers picked off, Boer fashion, by the American farmer-sharpshooters. His own collar was pierced by a bullet. The publicity of his defeat, however, was more than compensated at home by the fact that Lord George's trip to Kent had not been interfered with, and that nobody knew about the oversight of the dispatch. The policy of the English Government and Court for the next two years was simply concealment of Germain's neglect. Burgoyne's demand for an inquiry was defeated in the House of Commons by the court party; and when he at last obtained a committee, the king got rid of it by a prorogation. When Burgoyne realized what had happened about the instructions to Howe (the scene in which I have represented him as learning it before Saratoga is not historical: the truth did not dawn on him until many months afterwards) the king actually took advantage of his being a prisoner of war in England on parole, and ordered him to return to America into captivity. Burgoyne immediately resigned all his appointments; and this practically closed his military career, though he was afterwards made Commander of the Forces in Ireland for the purpose of banishing him from parliament.

The episode illustrates the curious perversion of the English sense of honor when the privileges and prestige of the aristocracy are at stake. Mr Frank Harris said, after the disastrous battle of Modder River, that the English, having lost America a century

99

ago because they preferred George III, were quite prepared to lose South Africa today because they preferred aristocratic commanders to successful ones. Horace Walpole, when the parliamentary recess came at a critical period of the War of Independence, said that the Lords could not be expected to lose their pheasant shooting for the sake of America. In the working class, which, like all classes, has its own official aristocracy, there is the same reluctance to discredit an institution or to "do a man out of his job." At bottom, of course, this apparently shameless sacrifice of great public interests to petty personal ones, is simply the preference of the ordinary man for the things he can feel and understand to the things that are beyond his capacity. It is stupidity not dishonesty.

Burgoyne fell a victim to this stupidity in two ways. Not only was he thrown over, in spite of his high character and distinguished services, to screen a court favorite who had actually been cashiered for cowardice and misconduct in the field fifteen years before; but his peculiar critical temperament and talent, artistic, satirical, rather histrionic, and his fastidious delicacy of sentiment, his fine spirit and humanity, were just the qualities to make him disliked by stupid people because of their dread of ironic criticism. Long after his death, Thackeray, who had an intense sense of human character, but was typically stupid in valuing and interpreting it, instinctively sneered at him and exulted in his defeat. That sneer represents the common English attitude towards the Burgoyne type. Every instance in which the critical genius is defeated and the stupid genius (for both temperaments have their genius) "muddles through all right," is popular in England. But Burgoyne's failure was not the work of his own temperament, but of the stupid temperament. What man could do under the circumstances he did, and did handsomely and loftily. He fell, and his ideal empire was dismembered, not through his own misconduct, but because Lord George Germain overestimated the importance of his Kentish holiday, and underestimated the difficulty of conquering those remote and inferior creatures, the colonists. And

King George and the rest of the nation agreed, on the whole, with Germain. It is a significant point that in America, where Burgoyne was an enemy and an invader, he was admired and praised. The climate there is no doubt more favorable to intellectual vivacity.

I have described Burgoyne's temperament as rather histrionic; and the reader will have observed that the Burgoyne of the Devil's Disciple is a man who plays his part in life, and makes all its points, in the manner of a born high comedian. If he had been killed at Saratoga, with all his comedies unwritten, and his plan for turning As You Like It into a Beggar's Opera unconceived, I should still have painted the same picture of him on the strength of his reply to the articles of capitulation proposed to him by the victorious Gates (an Englishman). Here they are:

Proposition.	Answer.
1. General Burgoyne's army being reduced by repeated defeats, by desertion, sickness, etc., their provisions exhausted, their military horses, tents and baggage taken or destroyed, their retreat cut off, and their camp invested, they can only be allowed to surrender as prisoners of war.	Lieut-General Burgoyne's army, however reduced, will never admit that their retreat is cut off while they have arms in their hands.
2. The officers and soldiers may keep the baggage belonging to them. The Generals of the United States never permit individuals to be pillaged.	Noted.
3. The troops under his Excellency General Burgoyne will be conducted by the most convenient route to New England, marching by easy	Agreed.

marches, and sufficiently provided for by the way.

4. The officers will be admitted on parole and will be treated with the liberality customary in such cases, so long as they, by proper behaviour, continue to deserve it; but those who are apprehended having broke their parole, as some British officers have done, must expect to be close confined.

There being no officer in this army under, or capable of being under, the description of breaking parole, this article needs no answer.

5. All public stores, artillery, arms, ammunition, carriages, horses, etc., etc., must be delivered to commissaries appointed to receive them.

All public stores may be delivered, arms excepted.

6. These terms being agreed to and signed, the troops under his Excellency's, General Burgoyne's command, may be drawn up in their encampments, where they will be ordered to ground their arms, and may thereupon be marched to the river-side on their way to Bennington.

This article is inadmissible in any extremity. Sooner than this army will consent to ground their arms in their encampments, they will rush on the enemy determined to take no quarter.

And, later on, "If General Gates does not mean to recede from the 6th article, the treaty ends at once: the army will to a man proceed to any act of desperation sooner than submit to that article."

Here you have the man at his Burgoynest. Need I add that he had his own way; and that when the actual ceremony of surrender came, he would have played poor General Gates off the stage, had not that commander risen to the occasion by handing him back his sword.

In connection with the reference to Indians with scalping knives, who, with the troops hired from Germany, made up about half Burgoyne's force, I may cite the case of Jane McCrea, betrothed to one of Burgoyne's officers. A Wyandotte chief attached to Burgoyne's force was bringing her to the British camp as a prisoner of war, when another party of Indians, sent by her betrothed, claimed her. The Wyandotte settled the dispute by killing her and bringing her scalp to Burgoyne. Burgoyne let the deed pass. Possibly he feared that a massacre of whites on the Canadian border by the Wyandottes would follow any attempt at punishment. But his own proclamations had threatened just what the savage chief executed.

BRUDENELL

Brudenell is also a real person. At least, an artillery chaplain of that name distinguished himself at Saratoga by reading the burial service over Major Fraser under fire, and by a quite readable adventure, chronicled, with exaggerations, by Burgoyne, concerning Lady Harriet Acland. Others have narrated how Lady Harriet's husband killed himself in a duel, by falling with his head against a pebble; and how Lady Harriet then married the warrior chaplain. All this, however, is a tissue of romantic lies, though it has been repeated in print as authentic history from generation to generation, even to the first edition of this book. As a matter of fact, Major Acland died in his bed of a cold shortly after his return to England; and Lady Harriet remained a widow until her death in 1815.

The rest of the Devil's Disciple may have actually occurred, like most stories invented by dramatists; but I cannot produce any documents. Major Swindon's name is invented; but the man, of course, is real. There are dozens of him extant to this day.

Notes

The notes in this edition are intended to serve the needs of overseas students as well as those of British-born users.

Inverted commas indicate references to stage directions.

You may notice in your text that Shaw does not use an apostrophe in words where we are accustomed to seeing it. Thus he gives us such forms as 'wont' and 'shant' instead of the usual 'won't' and 'shan't'. He had learnt from William Morris and other printers of fine books to consider the look of the page, and he argued that a page peppered with apostrophes was unnecessarily ugly. We may also see his assertive individualism in this and in his consistent preference for some American or old-fashioned spellings, as in 'honor' and 'shew'.

Act I

23 *'Mrs Dudgeon'*: the character's name suits her nature. The common noun, dudgeon, meaning 'bad temper', is oftenest met in the phrase, 'in high dudgeon'.

'New Hampshire': in the area of the United States of America known as New England. It had shared the same governor as Massachusetts until 1741, and its boundaries were only finally settled in 1764. The state assembly declared her independence from England in 1776, the year before the events of the play are supposed to have taken place. (See *Introduction*, pages xxviii–xxix.) *'Westerbridge'*: seems to be a fictitious place given a name typical of such a colonial area.

'prepossessing': attractive; not used only of physical attractiveness.

'barren forms . . . dead Puritanism': Shaw seems to imply that the religious faith which had inspired seventeenth-century Puritans to leave England for America had lost much of its freshness and fervour by the time of the War of Independence.

This view should not be taken as proved historical fact, but reveals Shaw's late nineteenth-century attitude to puritanical Christianity. (See *Introduction*, page xxxv.)

'pen': shut in.

'matron': housewife, married woman; rarely heard today in this sense.

'felony': legal term for a serious crime.

'license': allowed freedom. Shaw's spelling is normal American English today.

'licentious': generally used in a bad sense, describing behaviour lacking moral control.

'the seventh commandment': the one that forbids adultery. One of the ten commandments of the law given by God to Moses in the Old Testament (see *Exodus* 20:14).

'Presbyterian': not all the American colonists belonged to this branch of the Christian Church which has flourished more strongly in Scotland and Northern Ireland than in the rest of the British Isles. The name refers to the system of Church government, not by bishops supervising parish clergy and themselves subject to archbishops (as in the Church of England), but by councils of lay members of the congregation, called 'elders', meeting together with the minister, on a local level; and by a central council, the presbytery, consisting of all the clergy and lay delegates, responsible for general church policy and for ordaining the ministers chosen by local congregations. The official beliefs of Presbyterianism are derived from John Calvin (1509–64) who founded and strictly governed his church in Geneva. In this tradition, the law, the code of social and personal behaviour, was based on the Word of God, accessible in the Bible to all who could read. Calvin taught that salvation depended on faith, not on good works. Calvin's teaching may help us to understand the character of Mrs Dudgeon.

'more by their own weight ... will': reflection on the fact that the rebellion of the American colonies did not start as an attempt to get free of English rule, but resistance to English policies was

so widespread that it took on the proportions of a revolution.
'*the Rights of Man*': title of a work published in 1791–2 by
Tom Paine (1737–1809), a great champion of republicanism
who emigrated from England to America in 1774. He became
involved in the French Revolution, and it was to this cause
that *The Rights of Man* was particularly addressed.

24 '*domestic altar of the fireplace*': this metaphor anticipates Dick
Dudgeon's recognition that a home may be 'almost holy'
(pages 56–57).

'*sconce*': candle-holder often bracketed to a wall. Sconces are
associated with churches, so Shaw may be continuing his
metaphor.

'*three doors*': this is a description of a stage set, not just of any
fictional room, and it is worth noting what use would be made
of each door in performance.

'*deductive*': drawing deductions.

'*stridulous*': used here by Shaw to mean harsh to the touch, but
usually signifying a harsh or grating sound.

'*sixteen or seventeen*': in the England of Shaw's day, a girl of this
age was regarded as not quite grown up. This is important to
the play, as it means that Essie is not eligible to be a romantic
heroine.

'*rent*': torn.

25 '*rudely*': roughly.

'*cowed*': subdued, frightened.

'*Christy*': the name, short for Christopher ('bearer of Christ')
is appropriate to the good brother in a religious family. See
Christy's own words (page 83): 'He's the bad brother: I'm the
good one.'

'*plaid*': with a pattern of checks.

'*peremptorily*': bossily.

26 '*phlegmatically*': coolly, without emotion.

'*soullessly indifferent*': Shaw presents Christy as a man close to
the animals he presumably works with and is often compared
to, and like them in his limited intelligence and lack of any
moral or spiritual sense.

'*stupent*': struck with amazement.

Nevinstown: another apparently fictitious place.

27 '*bovine*': like an ox.

'*railing*': scolding, complaining.

a man may . . . even if his father's dead: note the comic effect of this.

'*divine*': clergyman.

'*sanguine*': reddish, suggesting vigour and optimism.

28 '*recalcitrant*': obstinately resistant. There is humour in the combination of this word with 'resignation', recognizing how some people cling to their grievances.

Springtown: another fictitious location.

bear my cross: suffer like Christ on the way to His crucifixion; a familiar pious phrase that the character uses unthinkingly, but that Shaw uses with ironical effect in the context of the hanging of Timothy and Peter's long, laborious journey.

'*vindictively*': vengefully, getting her own back.

dissolute: commonly describes addicts of drink and promiscuous sex.

29 *We are told . . . punished:* Mrs Dudgeon can quote scripture to confirm her views with the readiness of a well-trained Presbyterian. The texts in question include: 'all the wicked will he destroy' (*Psalm* 145:20); many verses in *Proverbs*, especially in chapters 10–21; 'I will punish the world for *their* evil, and the wicked for their iniquity' (*Isaiah* 13:11).

Why should we do our duty . . .: this shows up the falseness of Mrs Dudgeon's Presbyterianism, based not on faith in God but simply on desire for reward in the next world. This makes a striking contrast with Dick Dudgeon's later willingness to give his life for another man. (See page 69: 'I can find no manner of reason for acting as I did', and the long speech on page 72.)

30 *the heart of man is deceitful above all things:* another quotation from the Bible, *Jeremiah* 17:9.

not worthy . . . latchet: reference to *St Mark* 1:7 and *St Luke* 3:16, the words spoken by John the Baptist concerning Christ, 'the latchet of whose shoes I am not worthy to loose'.

What else ... the woman I am?: this may be another ironical line, as we see a different meaning in it from the one Mrs Dudgeon intends. However, it is also open to the actress playing the part to treat this whole section as indicating the character's bitter self-knowledge; she knows that she has become twisted through being denied love, and that she hates Anderson because she envies his happiness in a loving marriage.

32 *'barnbrack':* Anglo-Irish word Shaw may have remembered from his childhood for a teacake with currants in it; compare the traditional English 'barmbrack' for a bun made with yeast.

'the snuff': the burnt part of the candle wick.

33 *civil:* polite.

34 *'edified':* improved by good advice.

35 *wrestles and plays games on Sunday:* regarded as sinful not only among the Puritans of earlier centuries (forbidden by statute in the England of Oliver Cromwell), but by very many religious folk in the reign of Queen Victoria, as those who were children in those days often recalled in later life. The Victorian Sunday is attacked in a famous chapter of Charles Dickens's novel, *Little Dorrit*, mentioned by Shaw in his Preface, page 19.

36 *'brown riding gaiters and yellow breeches':* the costume draws attention to the figure in performance of the play and adds to the visual interest of the scene. See *Introduction*, page xlii.

'bottle-nosed': discoloured nose suggests too much alcohol has been drunk.

'purse-proud': priding herself on the social position money gives her.

'derelict': abandoned; usually applied to buildings.

'reprobate': sinner; lost from divine grace, hence, semi-humorously, a rascal.

37 *equal before the Throne:* equal in the presence or sight of God; using a biblical expression that seems appropriate for those in the midst of a rebellion against the British monarchy, as it is appropriate to people who accept the democratic principle of Presbyterian church government.

'*graced ... by the morning sunlight*': nature, not religion, distinguishes Dick. Shaw's wording of this description is part of the view expressed through the play as a whole that natural goodness and honest conviction are superior to the strained morality that does not come from the heart.

38 '*sardonic*': mocking, scornful.

'*satirical*': making others seem ridiculous.

'*picturesquely*': Shaw certainly wanted Richard to look like a certain type of romantic hero whose careless dress is attractive, not slovenly. The possibility is left open that Richard as a character dresses carelessly with an eye to effect, as he seems deliberately to play a part that will provoke everyone else in this scene.

'*a fanatic*': religious mystic, or one who will stop at nothing in the service of a religious or political belief.

'*throws his hat ... wicket keeper*': Richard's sudden movements, taking others by surprise, are typical of the swashbuckling hero in romantic plays and films.

'*his lip ... dog tooth*': the villains of melodrama often adopted this conventionally sinister expression. Richard mocks his mother by exaggerating the part in which she has cast him. 'Canine' may be a more familiar name for the pointed dog tooth today – the tooth supposed to be elongated in vampires!

upright horsedealer: although Uncle Titus may carry on his profession in a perfectly respectable fashion, Dick certainly uses the words tauntingly with reference to the popular belief that horse dealers (like gipsies) are practised cheats.

'*overborne*': overcome, put down.

39 *unction*: spiritual influence (the effect supposed to follow from a ritual anointing with oil). Both 'unction' and the adjective 'unctuous' are often used to hint at hypocrisy – what Shakespeare calls the 'oily art to speak and purpose not'.

'*shocked into sincerity*': like his reaction to the realization that Judith Anderson is present, this suggests that Dick is playing a part elsewhere in this scene, determined to annoy the others by not behaving as they think he should.

NOTES

40 *'wrath'*: anger; the word is frequent in the language of the seventeenth-century version of the Bible.

'checkmated': outmanoeuvred in a battle of wits, as when playing chess.

'presidential': like the chairman of a meeting.

41 *without the consolations of the law:* Dick's variant on the conventional phrase, 'without the consolations of religion'.

For what we are about to receive . . . : many readers will recognize these words as part of a grace (prayer) spoken before a meal. Dick implies that the family are like schoolchildren with their minds more on the food than on the prayer.

Primrose: her maiden name confirms an earlier hint (page 30) that Mrs Dudgeon may have been a very different person before her loveless marriage.

an annuity: form of pension.

42 *I recommend her for her goodness and piety:* what follows indicates that Peter wrote this ironically, with his tongue in his cheek.

The fatted calf: allusion to the biblical parable of the Prodigal Son, *St Luke* 15:11–23.

43 *cock of the walk:* cheeky phrase pointing out Richard's triumph.

'the weight of the law on women': married women in England were not allowed to own property before a series of Acts of Parliament was passed between 1870 and 1887. Women were still fighting for many other equal rights when *The Devil's Disciple* was written.

'Mary Wollstonecraft': (1759–97), pioneering feminist, thinker and writer, whose best-known book was *A Vindication of the Rights of Women* (1792). She entered on a free relationship with the political philosopher, William Godwin (1756–1836). Their daughter, Mary, married the poet Shelley and made her own place in history as the author of *Frankenstein* (1818).

44 *'cleaving to':* sticking to; another biblical expression.

'draught': drink.

sermons: do not you interrupt mine: Shaw's technique is worth noting here. By warning us of something dull to follow, he is more likely to hold our attention by surprising us. At the same time, the parallel Dick suggests between the minister and himself introduces us to an idea central to the play: that the villain may have his own beliefs and morality distinct from those of the man we recognize as good.

45 *the Devil was my natural master ...:* see Shaw's Preface, pages 19–20, on 'diabolonian ethics'.

You should be burnt alive: in his later play, *Saint Joan*, Shaw puts forward the view that such cruelties are the work of people who lack imagination. Note how Judith reacts later when Dick is about to be executed.

Major Swindon: invented character, as Shaw says in his Notes to the play, representing a typical officer.

46 *King George:* George III (1738–1820); meaning here the British Government and its forces. Richard is a rebel against both God and the King, religious and secular authority.

The devil's baptism: in a traditional melodrama, especially in emphatic position at the end of the Act, these words would make it clear to the audience that Richard was going to be converted.

Act II

47 *'griddle':* or 'girdle'; attachment for grilling over the fire.

'American cloth': oil cloth, the earliest forerunner of modern fabrics treated to make their surfaces waterproof for wiping clean.

'chapped': made rough, like skin in cold weather.

'japanned': lacquered or varnished (a technique in which the Japanese have long excelled).

'trencher': flattish dish or plate, made of wood or metal (often pewter), in common use in the seventeenth and eighteenth centuries.

'oak press': old form of wardrobe.

48 *'drugget':* floor covering of coarse fabric.

'mezzotint ... copperplate: prints produced by methods of

engraving, older than photographic reproduction.

'Raphael's St Paul preaching at Athens': the picture has a religious subject, but also indicates the Andersons' appreciation of art, as it is one of the masterpieces of a great Italian painter of the Renaissance period.

'rococo': style marked by extravagant ornament and fashionable through much of the eighteenth century; the finest examples were usually French.

'Mr Philip Webb and his disciples': Webb (1831–1915), Norman Shaw (1831–1912) and Sir Edward Lutyens (1869–1944) were architects who re-established what is known as the English Vernacular style in the houses they designed, inspired by the rural cottages and farmhouses of earlier centuries.

'the town clock strikes': from this point on, Shaw uses a sense of the passage of time to build up tension.

49 *King George:* George III did not go to America. Anderson uses his name to denote the British troops.

50 *what death must mean for a man like that:* according to a traditional belief, which many Christians have had difficulty in accepting, unrepentant sinners spend eternity in Hell.

51 *how like hate is to love:* this observation prepares us for Judith's change of attitude to Richard.

tax: try, put pressure on.

52 *stands on . . . ceremony:* behaves with formal politeness.

'cynically': in a disillusioned way, believing the worst of others.

53 *'an ironical bow':* acknowledging that the minister's 'whoever it belongs to' puts him neatly in his place as no more valuable than anyone else.

break bread: the biblical expression recalls the last supper of Christ with his disciples, ritually repeated by Christian congregations at Holy Communion.

desire to have you for my enemy: Richard evidently understands what Anderson was explaining to Judith before his arrival. Compare William Blake's saying, 'Opposition is true friendship', which Bernard Shaw turned into: 'I love my best friend./And who is that, pray?/My bravest enemy. That is the man who keeps me up to the mark', in his later play, *Major Barbara*. (See *Introduction*, page xxviii.)

54 *If all my enemies ... the best Christian:* Dick's compliment refers to Christ's commandment, 'Love your enemies' (*St Matthew* 5:44; *St Luke* 6:27).

55 *'disconcerted':* put out, embarrassed.

being a man ... being a woman: elsewhere, notably in his earlier play, *The Philanderer*, Shaw mocks the acceptance of sexual stereotypes, 'manly men' and 'womanly women', but such conventional simplifications are basic to melodrama. Compare Judith's words, 'I am only a woman ... suffer' (page 64).

56 *You are yourself again: so is Richard:* punning on a famous theatrical line, 'Conscience avaunt! Richard's himself again', from the popular eighteenth-century version of Shakespeare's *Richard III* made by Colley Cibber (1671–1757), often retained in nineteenth-century productions of the play. Richard III and Dick Dudgeon are two variant examples of the villain as hero of a play.

56–7 *not in my nature ... to be domesticated ... almost holy:* Shaw explored the attraction to an ideal of home life and the family felt by one who finally rejects it in another of the *Three Plays for Puritans, Candida*, where the young poet, Eugene Marchbanks, is – like Richard Dudgeon – an outsider looking at a happy marriage.

58 *a man of my cloth:* this conventional description of a clergyman has ironic force here, when it is truly the coat that makes the minister.

thank you kindly: Dick brings out everything gentlemanly in himself in acting the part of the minister.

59 *a game one:* plucky one (like a fighting cock).

to a bin: dialect version of 'to have been'.

Muffle the drums: giving a funereal sound.

'They file out quickly': Shaw's original manuscript of the play indicates that the drumming should continue until the curtain rises again, *'after a brief interval'*, to show Anderson's return. In

a modern production, it is probable that the lights would go down for a moment to denote the passage of time, instead of a curtain being brought down. Either way, the break should be minimal.

64 *my dearest is talking nonsense:* Judith may well attract more sympathy at this point than anywhere else in the play. The whole scene with Anderson shows similarities to a passage in the noted feminist play, *A Doll's House*, by Henrik Ibsen (1828–1906), when the young wife, Nora, is hoping that her husband will live up to her idealization of him and make an heroic self-sacrifice.

65 *hanged like that at his age!:* there is a touch of comic bathos, or anti-climax, in this sentence, comparable with the comic juxtaposition in Christy's 'a man may make a remark about the weather even if his father's dead' (Act I, page 27). Shaw is beginning to change the mood of the scene at this point.

'choleric': furiously angry.

66 *dying to save you:* this brings out the Christ-like quality of Dick's behaviour.

Blood an' owns!: soldier's blasphemous oath, 'by Christ's blood and wounds' (received at His crucifixion).

'powder horn': container for gunpowder, made of horn.

67 *Can we pray Swindon's rope ... neck?:* hardly a professional clergyman's response, but it is similar to a famous Puritan's – Oliver Cromwell's – soldierly practicality, illustrated in his saying, 'Trust in God and keep your powder dry'.

Act III

68 *'a little empty panelled waiting room':* Shaw's manuscript of the play indicates that this is a front scene, to be acted at the front of the stage, while the setting for the next scene is already in place, but concealed.

kep ... slep: dialect forms of 'kept' and 'slept'.

Bridewell: prison; it was originally the name of a hospital, which became 'a house of correction', at St Bride's Well in London.

mum: for 'ma'am' (madam).

spoil five: card game in which a player must win at least three out of five possible tricks, or the game is 'spoiled'.

spent it among us: buying them drinks.

'perverse': because it suits ill with the circumstances and her mood.

'raffish gallantry': the mock courtliness of manner that riff-raff, or down-at-heel scoundrels, may put on.

69 *General Burgoyne:* John Burgoyne (1723–92), actual English General involved in the War of American Independence. In his Note on Burgoyne which follows the play (pages 97–103), Shaw refers to his chief source of information, a book by Edward Barrington de Fonblanque, published in 1876. In attaching the nickname, 'Gentlemanly Johnny', to Burgoyne, Shaw drew attention to the qualities and values he wanted to represent in this character: the virtues and faults of the aristocrat, and he was delighted to find these amply illustrated in Fonblanque's book. In fact, Burgoyne's insistence on encumbering his army with an enormous amount of baggage, including a huge quantity of champagne and a silver service for regular formal dinners, added to his difficulties in the American campaign.

in Portugal: Burgoyne took part in the Seven Years' War, when France and Spain invaded Portugal, with which Britain was in alliance. He was responsible for capturing Alcantara in 1762.

70 *'gallantly':* playing the gentleman, with more of generous politeness than frankness in his answer.

by changing clothes with me: there are a number of popular legends of prisoners who escape in women's clothing, through the help of a wife or sweetheart; one of the best-known examples concerns the escape of the Earl of Nithsdale from the Tower of London after his part in the Jacobite rising of 1715.

cow: subdue.

men . . . notions . . . women see the folly: Dick recognizes that there are two sides to the question, both valid. This is a way of thinking that systematically takes into account the truth in opposed arguments – a characteristic of Shaw's work.

'*Vehemently*': forcefully, passionately.

The only man I have any right to kill: in fact, orthodox Christianity regards suicide as a sin.

71 '*divining the truth*': understanding that she has fallen in love with him.

72 *the same for any other man*: compare Anderson's earlier words to Dick, 'a man's life is worth saving, whoever it belongs to' (page 53). On this impartiality, see *Introduction*, page xxxiv.

73 '*G.R.*': Georgius Rex (King George). It is more likely that the colonists' traditional loyalty is still shown in the trappings of their Town Hall than that the British troops have brought and put up the curtains. It makes an imposing stage set, of course, and aptly symbolizes established authority, with which the play is much concerned.

'*maroon*': shade of dark red, sometimes called royal purple.

'*successful comedies*': *The Maid of the Oaks* (1775) and *The Heiress* (1786).

'*apprehensive*': seems to be used here in the sense of 'quick to understand', rather than the more usual 'fearful'.

74 *profane language*: swearing.

75 *writing a melodrama*: this is an anachronism; not until the beginning of the nineteenth century did plays of this kind, and so called, begin to be written. With this sarcasm, attacking Swindon's unthinking jingoism, Burgoyne distances himself from the kind of play Shaw has brought him into. In fact, with the introduction of Burgoyne, *The Devil's Disciple* moves further away from conventional melodrama. See *Introduction*, pages xxxix–xli.

Hessians, Brunswickers, German dragoons: the armies of the Hanoverian kings of England continued to employ mercenary troops from the German states. A dragoon is a cavalry soldier.

dissenter: rather contemptuous name for someone belonging to a sect that has separated itself from the established church.

76 *'The uniforms ... regiments'*: useful instructions for a stage manager, not just historical information. Shaw obviously wants quite a crowd of 'extras' who will make an audience on stage for Dick's trial.

sit at the feet of Gamaliel: the expression comes from the Bible, *Acts* 22:3. Gamaliel is identified in *Acts* 5:34 as 'a Pharisee ... a doctor of the law, had (held) in reputation among all the people'.

77 *As a matter of form then, my name ....:* for a 'bad' man, Dick has an unexpected reluctance to tell lies. The effect of dramatic irony, arising from the superior knowledge shared by an audience in the theatre, is also worth noting.

I never expect a soldier to think: need not imply that soldiers are stupid men, but that the disciplining of men to be soldiers involves clamping down on freedom of thought and question. ('Ours not to reason why' is the statement the poet Tennyson put into the mouths of the soldiers who died in the Charge of the Light Brigade, during the Crimean War.)

79 *I object to Lord North's robbing me*: Lord North (1732–92) was the English Prime Minister from 1770 to 1782 who continued the attempt to tax the American colonists directly as well as indirectly, when they were not represented in the English Parliament, and so provoked the riots that turned into the War of Independence.

pig-headed lunatic: not just a vague insult; Shaw seems to give his characters foreknowledge that George III was to go insane in 1788 and, after a period of recovery, spent his last years as, in the poet Shelley's words, 'An old, mad, blind, despised and dying king'.

'stentorian': of a powerful voice (from the name of a legendary herald in the Trojan War).

80 *'sick with horror'*: Shaw needs Judith on stage, crying out at this point, to keep the audience reminded of the realities behind the banter, in this scene.

black cap: customarily put on by trial judges when passing sentence of death.

117

do it like a gentleman: the moral ideal of the gentleman – and of the lady – was much discussed at the end of the nineteenth century and in the first years of the twentieth, a period when many people had ceased to be religious believers and the saintly ideal seemed irrelevant.

murder in a red coat: Shaw's realism led him to insist that killing in war was still murder. He was not a pacifist, but objected to moral pretentiousness aimed at concealing the squalid truth about warfare.

82 *Dispatches:* Shaw renews and complicates the tension by keeping us aware of events happening elsewhere.

83 *zany:* clown

85 *understrapper:* underling, inferior.

87 *Quebec ... New York ... Albany:* this refers to actual history, the march of Burgoyne's army, in the summer of 1777, from Canada into the Hudson Valley, aiming at the isolation of New England from the other American colonies.

General Howe: Sir William Howe (1729–1814), the commander-in-chief of the English forces in America at this time. Although there was a plan for Burgoyne and Howe to meet at Albany, it was not Howe but General Clinton who was expected to arrive from New York. Through a confusion of orders from London, Howe was engaged in a sea expedition to Chesapeake Bay. It is possible that Bernard Shaw deliberately took liberties with historical facts for the sake of greater simplicity and to keep the focus on the better-known Howe, whose name was more likely to be familiar to readers and audiences than Clinton's.

Jobbery: using public office for private gain.

Red Tape: official formalities obstructing efficiency. The phrase comes from the red (pink) tape used to tie up documents. See Shaw's Note (page 99) pointing out that Burgoyne's realization of what had happened is not historical.

Still in New York: the delay of General Clinton, expected from New York, left Burgoyne with inadequate forces to oppose the

Americans on 7 October 1777, supposedly soon after the events in this play. The result was a severe defeat for the English.

Saratoga: Burgoyne surrendered to General Gates (1728–1806) at Saratoga, in New York State, on 17 October 1777.

88 *'advertizers and examples of crime':* these punishments were supposed to warn by example, so that others might not imitate the crimes; but Shaw's choice of words fits in with his general attitude to judicial punishment. He gave one of his essays the title, *The Crime of Imprisonment*, and argued that prisons were evil institutions and that, as long as they existed, it was impossible to draw genuine moral distinctions between those behind bars and the rest who put them there. He believed it was more humane to kill dangerous human beings as dangerous wild animals are killed, without ceremonious hypocrisy. See Richard's long speech, page 90.

'beadle': parish constable.

Dress: draw up in formation.

Some o youll ... Hoosians ... talkin German ... argufying: Shaw indicates through the Sergeant's speech that he belongs to a lower social class than the other officers.

89 *dress up:* line up.

'the Dead March of Saul': this very slow, impressively solemn music from the oratorio, *Saul*, by George Frederick Handel (1685–1750), is usually played at state funerals. It would contribute powerfully to the mood of this scene.

'surplice': white linen vestment, worn over a cassock; like black cap and red coat, another interesting use of costume.

90 *Man that is born of woman hath – :* the opening words of the Burial Service in the Church of England *Book of Common Prayer*.

'Thou shalt not kill': one of the Ten Commandments (*Exodus* 20:13; *Deuteronomy* 5:17). St Paul's *Epistle to the Romans*, 13:9, points out that these are summed up in Christ's commandment to love one another.

92 *'falls on her knees in prayer':* Shaw arranges this touching scene as if for a Victorian picture.

that will do very nicely: Shaw wrote to Mrs Richard Mansfield that this comment of Burgoyne's should have a 'cruel effect'. He evidently wanted Burgoyne's almost inhuman detachment to appear in his manner here. However, it could be argued that the words express humane relief that there is no need for the soldiers to remove Judith by force.

'chronometer': imposing word for a watch, used more frequently in the past than today.

93 *'enemies in the gate':* another biblical phrase (*Psalm* 127:5).

an American clock: on this rather feeble joke and what follows, see *Introduction*, page xxxviii.

ahead of you already: anachronistic reference to the difference of time (5 hours) regularly observed today between the eastern USA and Britain. Not until the late nineteenth century was time in North America officially related to time at Greenwich, and zone-times throughout the world set from Greenwich Mean Time were not established until the present century.

94 *commander of the militia:* Anderson seems to have been promoted as rapidly as Mrs Dudgeon's health has declined!

Suffer and be faithful to the death: from the *Book of Common Prayer*; compare 'be thou faithful unto death', *Revelations* 2:10.

the thunder of the captains and the shouting: biblical expression for 'battle', taken from *Job* 39:25.

wag his pow: humorous use of a Scottish expression in which 'pow' means 'head' (compare 'poll'). *The English Dialect Dictionary* records 'wag yer pow in her faither's poopit' from a work published in 1869.

95 *without a Conquest:* referring, of course, to the Norman Conquest, to which the most aristocratic English families trace back their titles.

Come and settle the matter at my quarters: so the War of Independence is very cursorily disposed of, when Shaw has worked out his theme and wants to bring his play to an end.

'British Grenadiers': probably now the best-known of British regimental marches. The tune is of eighteenth-century origin.

96 *'Yankee Doodle':* the tune is believed to have been composed in

1755 by a surgeon in Lord Amherst's army in America. Originally intended as mockery of the native American troops, it was adopted by the New Englanders as a national march. So it is both historically and dramatically appropriate here.

'*They shake hands*': matter-of-fact and friendly, a contrast to the expected theatrically conventional kiss.

Study questions

Act I

1　In what ways is Dick Dudgeon a bad man?
2　What impression of Anthony Anderson do you get from Act I?
3　On his first entrance, Dick *'throws his hat to Christy with a suddenness that makes him jump like a negligent wicket keeper'*. If you are studying the play in class, try acting out the scene that follows as if it were a ball game, Dick suddenly pouncing to catch the others off their guard, while they watch him intently, hoping to be ready for his attacks. Note that some of the characters are better players than others.

Act II

4　Compare and contrast Richard Dudgeon, as he appears in Act II, with Anthony Anderson. Does each of them change greatly during this Act?
5　How does Shaw prepare, in Act II, for the soldiers' mistake in taking Richard for the minister?
6　'I daresay your love helps him to be a good man, just as your hate helps me to be a bad one.' (Richard, page 57) Do you think this idea goes any way to explain the change that appears in Richard in Act II and Act III?

Act III

7　What is your impression of General Burgoyne? Do you find him an attractive character, or repellant?
8　How does Shaw show us the emotional stress Richard is under, in the trial scene? Look for changes of style in the way he speaks.

9 What effects does Shaw achieve by having Judith present at the trial and then following Richard to his execution?

10 Lester Cohen's script for a film of *The Devil's Disciple* omitted Judith's lines (Act II, page 80):

> Is it nothing to you what wicked thing you do if only you do it like a gentleman? Is it nothing to you whether you are a murderer or not, if only you murder in a red coat?

Write a letter, as Bernard Shaw's secretary on behalf of Mr Shaw, to David O Selznick, head of RKO, protesting against Cohen's script on the evidence of this cut.

11 'More of a show than a proper trial.' Do you agree with this comment on the second scene of Act III?

12 The ending of the 1959 film included a clear hint of future romance between Essie and Dick. Do you think Shaw has left the way open for this? Would it alter your impression of the character of Dick Dudgeon?

Characters and character relationships

13 Consider the importance of the ages Shaw gives to Essie, Judith, Dick and Anthony Anderson. How does age affect the relationships between them?

14 What do you make of Dick Dudgeon's attitude to women?

Dramatic structure and dialogue

15 Consider Shaw's placing of intimate scenes (or passages) in relation to public scenes. How does this add to the interest and effectiveness of the play as a whole?

16 Look at Richard's long speech to Judith (beginning 'If I said – to please you – that I did what I did ...') in the first scene of Act III (page 72). Read it aloud. Consider:

(a) How does it differ in style from everyday conversation?
(b) What means has Shaw used, in writing the lines, to give weight to what is being said?
(c) What qualities in this speech might lead you to suspect that the author had been a public speaker?
(Alternatively, you could apply these questions to Anderson's speech beginning 'Sir; it is the hour of trial ...' later in the same Act – page 94.)

The importance of stagecraft

17 Consider some of the uses of stage costume made by Shaw in *The Devil's Disciple*, in the plot, for characterization and emotional effect, and to demonstrate ideas.
18 Consider how Shaw wants music and visual effects to serve his dramatic purposes (e.g. by setting up a mood, or creating a striking stage image).

General questions

19 Which do you think is, finally, the hero of the play: Dick Dudgeon or Anthony Anderson?
20 Would you describe *The Devil's Disciple* as a religious play?